THE
SAS

AT CLOSE
QUARTERS

SIDGWICK & JACKSON
LONDON

THE
SAS
AT CLOSE QUARTERS

STEVE CRAWFORD

First published in Great Britain in 1993
by Sidgwick & Jackson Limited

ISBN 0 283 06183-9

Printed and bound in Great Britain by
BPCC Hazell Books Ltd
Member of BPCC Ltd

Sidgwick & Jackson Limited
18-21 Cavaye Place
London SW10 9PG

Editorial and Design: Brown Packaging

I would like to take the opportunity to thank the following
people, without whose help and support this book would not
have been possible:

Karen, for being my inspiration.

Kevin, my training partner, for giving me the motivation to
keep going when I was ready to give up.

Simon, for his help with the design, and for keeping calm
when the courier failed to arrive.

David, for his patience during the hours spent on the
telephone, when I was trying to understand what must have
been extremely straightforward to him.

Already published excerpts taken from:

Soldier 'I' SAS by Michael Paul Kennedy, published by
Bloomsbury Publishing Ltd (1990)

One of the Originals by Johnny Cooper, published by Pan
Books Ltd (1991)

One Man's SAS by Lofty Large, published by William
Kimber & Co. Ltd (1987)

The Quiet Soldier by Adam Ballinger, published by
Chapmans Publishers Ltd (1992)

Shoot to Kill by Michael Asher, published by Penguin
Books (1990)

David Stirling by Alan Hoe, published by Little, Brown
and Company (UK) Ltd (1992)

Picture credits
Anne Bolt: 143; **Brown Packaging:** 6, 45, 50-
51, 64-65, 66, 67, 69, 70, 74, 76-77, 78, 79, 92-
93, 112-113, 114-115, 116-117, 140, 174-175,
182, 187, 189; **IWM:** 18-19, 21, 23, 24, 25, 26,
48-49, 54-55, 62-63; **Pacemaker Press:** 132-
133, 135, 136-137, 147; **Press Association:** 72-
73; **Private Collection:** 2-3, 14, 15, 16-17, 32-
33, 37, 80-81, 83, 85, 89, 91, 97, 98-99, 100-
101, 102-103, 104-105, 107, 108-109, 110-111,
119, 121, 126, 138-139, 153, 154, 158-159, 162-
163, 164, 166-167, 168-169, 177, 178-179, 184,
185; **Tony Rogers:** 8-9, 10, 13, 53, 58, 59, 60-
61, 123, 124-125, 129, 151; **SAS Regimental
Association:** 29, 31; **Telegraph Colour
Library:** 38-39; **TRH Pictures:** 35, 43, 46,
148-149, 160-161; **US DoD:** 170-171, 172-173,
180-181

Artworks
Terry Hadler: 40-41, 56-57, 86-87, 130-131,
144-145, 156-157; **Keith Harmer:** 75

**Front cover: The SAS storms the Iranian Embassy,
May 1980.
Previous pages: A special forces sniper takes aim
with an L96A1 sniping rifle.
Back cover: SAS troopers in Borneo, early 1960s.**

CONTENTS

PREFACE

Of all the elite military units in the world, perhaps the most famous is Britain's Special Air Service. The reason for this is because it has been very successful in its operations since it was formed in the North African desert by David Stirling in 1941. Now, in this book, and for the first time, individual SAS soldiers talk frankly and openly about those operations.

This book is not a detailed history of the Special Air Service Regiment; rather, it seeks to provide the reader with an insight into what it's like to be an SAS soldier at the sharp end of war: cross-border raids in Borneo, fighting terrorists in the deadly 'bandit country' of South Armagh, or operating behind the lines in Iraq during the Gulf War. The reader will learn what it's like to be in combat: the adrenalin rush before the assault on the Iranian Embassy, firefights with Indonesian troops in Borneo, shooting up enemy aircraft on Pebble Island during the Falklands War, and the ambushing of Scud missile batteries in Iraq. What is painted is a picture of men who are elite in every way, but who are also modest and go about their tasks with a quiet confidence and a sense of humour. From the rigours of Selection, the freezing cold of the Falklands, to the scorching heat of Oman, this is their story using their words.

For reasons of security and personal safety, the names of most of the soldiers talking in this book cannot be given. This is only proper: some are still serving in the Regiment, while others, though no longer SAS soldiers, are engaged in other covert activities.

The mark of excellence: the SAS winged dagger badge.

SELECTION

'I have a mental blue-print of the ideal SAS man. No one fits it exactly but, when I look at a man and listen to him he must come close to it.'

Lieutenant-Colonel 'Paddy' Mayne, 1944

This chapter illustrates how the concepts laid down by the founders of the Regiment in the early 1940s concerning the type and calibre of recruits and the overall ethos of the SAS has remained unchanged through five decades. It reveals how the stringent selection and training routines currently operated by the SAS continue a legacy of excellence that was established during World War II and, later, in Malaya and Oman. The common denominator of the Regiment has been, and will always be, its individual soldiers. They are special, a breed apart.

Individual soldiers of the Special Air Service must possess certain qualities that will enable them to operate effectively as part of a small team behind enemy lines, often for weeks at a time, and devoid of substantial support services. What are these qualities? The guiding principles of the Regiment were laid down by its founder, Lieutenant-Colonel David Stirling, over 50 years ago: to engage in the never-ending pursuit of excellence, to maintain the highest standards of self-discipline in all aspects of daily life, to tolerate no sense of class, and all ranks to possess humility and humour.

The SAS has possibly the most arduous military selection course in the world. As well as physical stamina, all potential recruits must have high levels of personal initiative and intelligence.

Above: The ability to keep going when others give up is one of the hallmarks of an SAS soldier.

SAS soldiers have always fought in small units. In this they are no different from other troops of the British Army. An infantry section, for example, usually comprises around eight men. However, the major difference between conventional and special forces such as the SAS is that the former nearly always operate within larger groups and can call upon support services: aircraft, artillery, tanks and even naval support. But there are very few instances of SAS soldiers operating together in large numbers, the exception being the closing stages of World War II. Between March and May 1945, for example, two squadrons from 1 and 2 SAS, comprising a total of 430 men and 75 jeeps, undertook short-range reconnaissance for the British 21st Army Group east of the Rhine. However, this mission, Operation 'Archway', was an exception; most of the time SAS soldiers fight in small groups, and often behind enemy lines.

Of all the qualities looked for in an aspiring SAS soldier, self-discipline is perhaps the most important, followed closely by high levels of mental and physical stamina. The desire to get the job done in a no-nonsense fashion, and without acclaim, has always been high on the list of SAS priorities. Soon after the establishment of the first SAS base camp at Kabrit, Egypt, in late 1941, David Stirling reminded his first batch of recruits:

'There will be no bragging or swanking in the Cairo or Alexandria bars and that goes for scrapping too. Any energy you have for fighting will be directed at the enemy. Make no mistake, anyone who doesn't fit in will leave – there will be no second chances. Captain Lewes will be in sole charge of training and that includes my own. It's going to be tough because we have to be fit for the job we're going to do. If anyone has sensible and constructive comments to make on training, or any other operational subject, then make it. We are all here to learn.'

Some 30 years later, Michael Asher encountered the same attitude when he first met the soldiers of 23 SAS, one of the part-time SAS Regiments:

'There were no loud-mouths or bar-soldiers. There was a palpable sense of quiet determination about them, a seriousness which dealt with each obstacle as an interesting problem. There was no aspect of training which was too trivial to examine in detail: nothing was waved aside in the pressure of achieving the goal. These SAS men looked very fit, but as a matter of course rather than as a means to prove themselves "tough" or superior. You could tell at a glance that they were above "beasting" for its own sake. They were not truculent or sadistic, as the Paras had been. You could see that they might kill easily, but never for the love of it.'

To prepare SAS soldiers for the type of warfare they will undertake, the Regiment operates a rigorous elimination process, one that is designed to weed out the unsuitable quickly. The principles of Selection Training were first laid down by 'Jock' Lewes during World War II, and then refined further by Lieutenant-Colonel John Woodhouse during the 1950s. Johnny Cooper, one of the first recruits to the SAS, sums up the training ethos of the Special Air Service during World War II:

'Jock instilled into us that the end product of our training was for us to become independent in every way, operating either alone or in very small groups. We would have to develop an ingrained self-confidence in our ability to navigate across featureless terrain without any back-up whatsoever and using maps that gave little or no detail. We would have to survive on minimum sustenance and to control the use of food and water during the hot periods of the day, using the cover of darkness for offensive activity.'

The current Selection Training programme of the SAS is conducted by Training Wing, 22 SAS,

and lasts for one month. It is divided between a three-week build-up period and Test Week, which is the culmination of Selection. The course, on paper at least, sounds reasonably straightforward. It begins with a set of road runs which increase in length during the first week. This is followed by a series of marches over the Black Mountains and Brecon Beacons of South Wales to test the students' proficiency in map reading and navigation: each man is given a bergen, a map and a compass, and is then given a grid reference for the first rendezvous. When he reaches the first rendezvous he is told the next one, and so on. All the time he is being watched and assessed by the training staff. The climax of Selection is Test Week, the culmination of which is the notorious 60km navigation exercise over the Brecon Beacons, nicknamed 'Long Drag' or 'Fan Dance'. This must be completed within 20 hours, regardless of the weather, for the recruit to pass Selection.

There is no doubt that Selection is extremely tough, the more so because each man is on his own. There are no mates around him to encourage him or deter him from giving up, there are no screaming NCOs issuing threats and encouragement; there is only the individual's own drive and determination to keep him going. For some this isn't enough: they drop out and are returned to their parent unit (RTU'd in British Army parlance). This doesn't necessarily mean they are bad soldiers, far from it, but only the very best get into the SAS – men who have the will to keep on going when their bodies are screaming for them to stop, and ones whose minds are still able to function in such circumstances. One SAS trooper remembers the sense of isolation:

'There is no shouting or screaming, no encouragement or excesses; you pass or fail on the merits of your own physical and mental abilities.
'We tumbled out of bed at the crack of dawn, paraded at 0630 hours in three ranks and waited for the instructor to arrive with the day's programme. Everyone wears their own beret at the start of the day, but puts it away when the

course moves onto the Brecons or other training areas in the region. The first two weeks of Selection are when the instructors pick out the "lambs": the physically weak who they feel will not make the required times. They also weed out those whose "character" doesn't fit, for example those who are noisy and are referred to as being nothing more than a "mouth on a stick". All the unsuitable ones are quickly got rid of.

'In the old days those who were fit but unsuitable found themselves facing "sickeners": a physical punishment used to break their morale and make them quit. One involved being "issued" with several large rocks by training staff at a checkpoint. The instructors would then call at the next checkpoint to make sure the recruit was still carrying them. The worst, however, was the removal of boot laces halfway through a long march. At the end of the march the recruit's feet would be swollen and blistered like you wouldn't believe. But now this has all been done away with, and today if you're not wanted you are quietly pulled into the office and given a rail warrant. Within an hour you are gone, and all the other blokes see when they get back is an empty bed.

'There were 142 hopefuls at the start of my course, but this started to drop within the first few hours as the instructors began to siphon out those who were, in their opinion, "wasters". Once the course is up and running it's all about speed. In my previous unit I had been regarded as a very good runner, and during my training for Selection had prided myself on the weights I carried and the speed I worked at. In infantry battalions the training staff often take the speed of the slowest man as a marker, provided he is running fast enough to meet the required time, the concept being to get everyone to end up as a group. In the SAS this is reversed. The Regiment uses the speed of the fastest man as a marker – it's not

interested in everyone finishing as a group – and as a result the pace of some marches is crippling.

'For me the worst was a 10km speed march with bergens, belt order and weapons. The pain in my legs and hips will always stay with me. My face was on fire, but I knew I couldn't give in. There is no point in approaching Selection with anything less than 100 per cent commitment with regard to getting through, whatever the cost. If you can do this you'll be alright, but any nagging distraction can be enough to make blokes quit, especially any problems with wives or girlfriends. Some blokes tell their partners they're going overseas for four weeks, which gives them total isolation to concentrate on the course.

'On Selection everyone is put into syndicates of four, and the instructors will usually give a few tips and make sure each man is in his best physical shape to have a "fair crack" at the course. Our instructor, a veteran who hailed from the west Midlands, waited until we all had serious blisters before paying us a visit one evening. Seeing for himself the shattered mess that our feet had become, he suggested we each buy a jar of vaseline, rub it into our feet and then put our socks back on. "That will solve it, no problem". And he was right.

'Such philanthropy tends to disappear on the hills, where the only important thing is getting to the next checkpoint on time. If you are late or your bergen looks light, an instructor will present you with a rock to add to your difficulties. The smart ones carry it until they are out of sight, then ditch it and pick up a fresh one before they get to the next checkpoint. It's all about keeping your mind working, you see. Those who don't use their initiative fall back and fail. I remember at the end of the course there were only 17 of us left, and we had only passed Selection: there was still Continuation to go.'

All SAS soldiers, regardless of the period they served in the Regiment, agree on the tough nature of Selection Training. Lofty Large passed the course in the 1950s:

> 'At the end I was fit to drop, completely smashed. Some had already dropped. We were told that was just a warm-up. Sure enough it was. My next trick, as far as I can remember, was a 35-mile hike, with 50lb on my back, all across country ("you will not use roads or bridges") which lasted nearly two days. We went from one RV (rendezvous) to another, never knowing which would be the last. I waded the River Wye twice and slept the night on the mountains, soaking wet and cold but too shattered to notice. We had to travel alone, if two men were caught walking together they risked RTU; the same if we were caught on roads or bridges.'

Above: All SAS soldiers receive intensive training in the use of weapons, such as this SA-80.

Nearly 20 years later two more aspiring SAS soldiers had to endure the rigours of Selection and Test Week. Michael Asher (23 SAS) confirms the importance of the brain still being able to function despite the body being in a state of total exhaustion:

> 'In addition to the 55-pound bergen, I now had to carry all the food and water I should consume on the way, plus an SLR rifle and 200 rounds of ammunition. The rifle had to be kept perfectly clean and operational at all times and carried at the ready no matter how exhausted I might be...In between marches we were expected to be alert enough to take in lessons. When all we wanted to do was to collapse on our beds, the RSM's dog-shark face would be thrust in front of us in some

smoky Nissen hut, explaining how to strip and assemble a Kalashnikov AK-47 assault rifle.'

In late 1941, Captain Fitzroy Maclean was having a similar experience in the Western Desert while preparing for the SAS's very first operation behind the lines:

'For days and nights on end we trudged interminably over the alternating soft sand and jagged rocks of the desert, weighed down by heavy loads of explosive, eating and drinking only what we could carry with us. In the intervals we did weapon training, physical training and training in demolitions and navigation.'

The motto of Training Wing is 'Train Hard, Fight Easy', meaning that all SAS soldiers will be as prepared for combat as possible. Those men who have passed through Selection successfully might add that SAS training is really a series of bloodless battles, whereas actual combat is just a bloody training session.' Soldier 'I' was another who went through the hell of Selection and the culminating 'Long Drag':

'I pushed across jagged stones, squelched through peat bogs, crushed through lime-green beds of young fern shoots and picked my way across stagnant pools of water by jumping from one clump of reeds to another. The olive oil on my socks didn't help this time; the friction in my boots felt like someone pushing a hot, razor-sharp file across the skin of my ankles. Backwards and forwards relentlessly with each step, sapping my will-power and determination, until it felt

Opposite: Parachuting is a major part of training. Below: When fully 'badged', SAS troopers go on to receive training in both troop and patrol skills. Being in a Boat Troop, for example, means mastering all aspects of amphibious warfare.

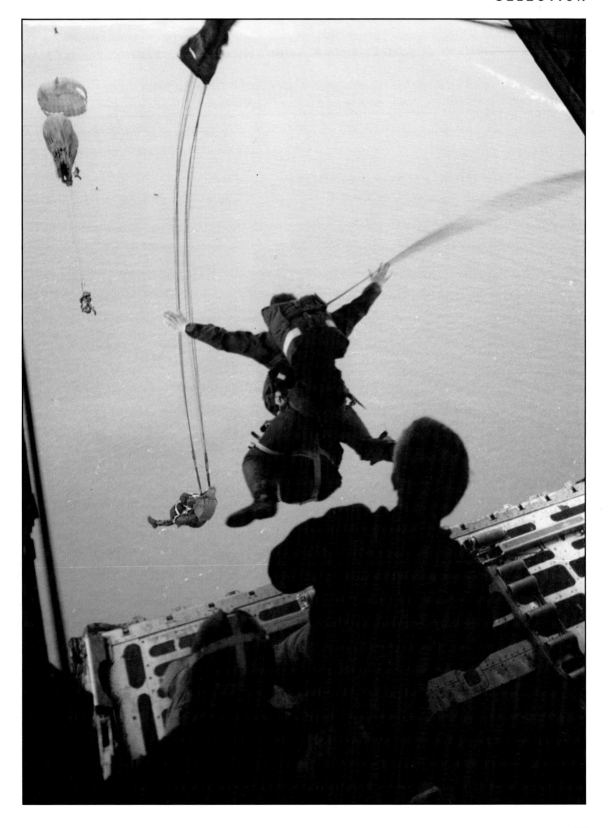

as if the file was sawing against raw bone. I kept repeating out aloud over and over again as the sun rose higher and hotter, "I've got this far, I'm fucked if I'm going to jack now!" I was overwhelmed by feelings of isolation and loneliness. I felt as though I was the only person for miles around. I must keep going. The sun was getting fiercely hot. It was one of those rare spring days that was a match for the best that summer could offer.

'Midday. I'd been going eight hours and I reckoned I was still less than half-way round the course. The sun was extraordinarily hot for the time of year. Just our fucking luck, I thought, on the very day we could have done with some cloud cover and a cool breeze. As I paused momentarily to get my bearing, my legs began to give way under the load of the bergen. My lungs felt raw, as if someone had thrust their fist down my throat and ripped a layer of skin off them. My facial expression became set in a glazed stare. What the fuck am I doing this for?, I asked myself. Do I really want to suffer like this? No answer came back. I scanned my brain

but could find no logic with which to talk myself into any more pain.'

Passing Selection Training means prospective SAS soldiers go on to Continuation Training, in which each man learns basic SAS skills to enable him to become an effective member of a four-man patrol (the smallest SAS operational unit). This entails learning standard operating procedures (SOPs), signalling, medicine, combat and survival skills, as well as negotiating a resistance-to-interrogation exercise. There then follows jungle training and a static-line parachuting course, after which those who are left become fully fledged members of 22 SAS Regiment. At any time the prospective recruit can be failed and RTU'd, a particularly cruel blow when one has undertaken six months of training and is so close to winning the famed winged dagger badge.

There is no doubt that becoming an SAS soldier means that the individual has become de facto an elite operative. However, in the never-ending pursuit of excellence which is the hallmark of the SAS, individual troopers are not allowed to rest on their laurels. There is no such thing as a fully trained SAS soldier. The Regiment sets great store by all its soldiers being multi-skilled individuals. This being the case, all its soldiers spend their SAS careers continually learning new skills. This means that four-man patrols are filled with multi-skilled individuals, which allows the unit to function effectively even if it has lost 25-50 per cent casualties.

Thus today's Special Air Service is composed of highly trained, skilled individuals who can undertake a wide variety of missions, from hostage-rescue operations to intelligence gathering deep behind enemy lines. In addition, there are many specialist units that provide logistic and intelligence back-up to the Regiment: an Army Air Corps special flight, an RAF Special Forces Flight, as well as the research and intelligence units based at the SAS's UK base at Hereford (Stirling Lines).

It is the proud boast of the SAS that its men can fight in any terrain anywhere in the world. This means continuous training in hostile regions.

THE EARLY YEARS

In its first two decades of existence, the SAS fought in many types of terrain, from the North African desert to the Malayan jungle.

During its formative years, the SAS didn't have the elaborate and comprehensive resources that it currently possesses, and there was no Selection. However, it did have its recruits – men who were physically and mentally tough. Such a person was Bob Bennett, one of David Stirling's 'Originals', who attests to the demands made upon him and his comrades:

'After a while, we began our parachute course. We started with jumping from platforms 12ft from the ground but then someone had the bright idea of getting us to leap off trucks moving at 30mph. After three attempts, we were all battered and bruised, so that was stopped. Our first live jump from two Bristol Bombay aircraft was cut short after two men were killed. That night we all went to bed with as many cigarettes as possible and smoked until morning. Next day, every man jumped; no one backed out. It was then that I realised that I was with a great bunch of chaps...Just before we went on the first mission, we did a four-day route march across the desert from Kabrit to Heliopolis airfield.'

A World War II SAS jeep kitted out for operations in North Africa. Equipped with Vickers 'K' and Browning machine guns, jeeps were put to devastating use in 1942-43 against Axis airfields.

That first mission mentioned by Bob Bennett was an attack by L Detachment, SAS, on two Axis airfields scheduled for 17 November 1941. It was designed to support Operation 'Crusader', the attempt of General Claude Auchinleck, Commander-in-Chief Middle East, to throw General Rommel's *Afrika Korps* out of Cyrenaica. The 65 SAS soldiers were dropped by parachute on the night of 16/17 November. However, it was a complete disaster, with the men and their equipment being widely scattered due to high winds. Several men were badly injured when they hit the ground and, as a result, the operation had to be abandoned. Despite this initial setback, the SAS continued to train for attacks on enemy airfields and supply depots behind enemy lines. David Stirling decided that henceforth his men would no longer use parachute drops as a means of getting to the target; instead they would be transported to their objectives by the vehicles of the Long Range Desert Group (LRDG).

This slight change in operational procedure brought immediate success: in December 1941 the SAS launched attacks against the enemy airfields at Sirte, Agheila, Tamit, Nofilia and Marble Arch. These actions resulted in the destruction of around 100 enemy aircraft. The new year brought even greater success, vindicating Stirling's belief in the effectiveness of small-sized groups operating behind the lines, as Fitzroy Maclean states:

'Working on these lines, David achieved a series of successes which surpassed the wildest expectations of those who had originally supported his venture. No sooner had the enemy become aware of his presence in one part of the desert than he was attacking them somewhere else. Never has the element of surprise, the key to success in all irregular warfare, been more brilliantly exploited. Soon the number of aircraft destroyed on the ground was well into three figures.'

What was it like for individual SAS soldiers engaged on these hit-and-run missions? Inevitably, no two operations were the same, but they all shared common characteristics. First, there was the trip to the target area. Transported by the trucks of the LRDG, the journey was usually uneventful, though constant watch had to be kept for enemy aircraft. Reg Seekings, one of the 'Originals', describes a typical trip in an LRDG truck in January 1942:

'Most of the time we were loaded to do the complete journey, which was why we needed well-run-in trucks. Everything was grossly overloaded. We'd carry food, water and petrol. We also carried ammunition. We needed lots of that...And we fed well. We got on to the LRDG ration scale which was different from the rest of the army. They had tinned fruit. They were really twenty-four-hour jobs, those patrols. You were covering as many miles a day as you possibly could, depending on the going...We were continually mending punctures...It was really tough going on those jobs. Good fun.'

Whether or not these missions were actually good fun is debatable. Nevertheless, they were highly effective, proving Stirling's point that small parties could achieve a far greater degree of success than the large-scale raids previously practised by the British in North Africa. When the target was reached, the actual action was less glamorous than might be expected. The idea, then as now, was to infiltrate the target, lay the explosives and then withdraw with as little fuss as possible (the very last thing troops operating behind the lines want to do is attract unnecessary attention).

In March 1942, a party of SAS soldiers raided an enemy airfield at Berka. The story of the operation is relayed by Bob Bennett:

'We hit the perimeter at about midnight and saw German sentries strolling along the road. As usual, we waited until they had walked by our position and then shot across the road into the trees on the other side. There, we split into two groups. I was with Paddy [Mayne], and we went for the bombers lying under the cover of the trees. We just walked down the line of aircraft lobbing Lewes bombs onto their wings. When the job was finished, Paddy and I sped out of the place.

'When we halted for a break, the bombers started to go up – it must have been about two hours as we were using time pencils of that duration. The Germans didn't seem to know what had happened: they were firing into the air or out to sea. In fact, it took them a heck of a long time to get wise.'

Bob Bennett gives the impression that destroying enemy aircraft was easy. And so it may have been at first, as the Germans and Italians were caught unawares by Stirling's men. However, airfield security was soon tightened, making it a lot more difficult to get at the aircraft. In addition, there was the constant worry that, having hit an airfield, the SAS would not make the rendezvous with the LRDG. If this happened the SAS soldiers were faced with a long trek through the desert back to base. One party that made such a journey was the one led by Bill Fraser in January 1943 after successfully attacking Marble Arch airfield. Having reached the rendezvous point but unaware that an LRDG patrol had been despatched to the wrong point, the SAS team waited. When it became clear that the LRDG was not going to arrive, the men decided to walk the 320km back to base. The training instigated by Jock Lewes came into its own. One of the group, Private Byrne, describes the journey:

'We took turns to lead, every one of us setting a cracking pace, determined to match each other's resolution. Weary beyond belief, we kept tramping on, stamping our feet into the soft desert sand and lifting them up again like automata, every step an effort...The sun burned into eyes from high overhead and was reflected up again from the sand. There was no escape from it and we longed for the luxury of sun glasses or a peaked cap. At dusk we dug holes in the sand, curled up in our blankets and tried to sleep.'

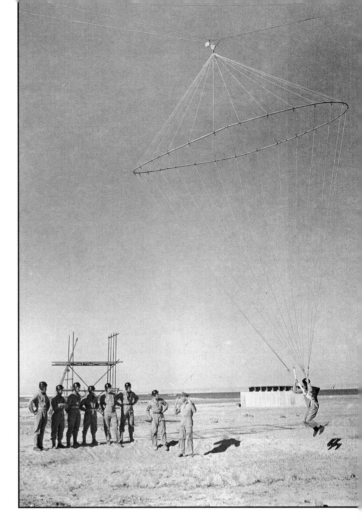

Above: Recruits undergoing parachute training at the SAS's first base at Kabrit, Egypt, in 1942.

The fact they made it back to base is testimony to the legendary stamina of SAS soldiers.

Mid-1942 witnessed a change in SAS battle tactics when Stirling's men used the US Willys jeep for the first time. The vehicles were heavily armed – twin Vickers 'K' machine guns mounted front and rear, and often supplemented with a .50in Browning heavy machine gun – and equipped for long-range desert operations: water condensers, sand mats, radios, metal wheel channels and spare ammunition. The jeeps were first used at Bagoush airfield in July 1942 to devastating effect. Johnny Cooper was one of those who took part in the raid:

'With all guns cocked we approached the silhouetted aircraft, and as we came alongside the first one, the Vickers 'K's opened up with a mixture of tracer, armour-piercing and explosive bullets. I was manning the forward single Vickers and our rear gunner had the twins. David [Stirling] was encouraging us from the driving seat and we could tell from his voice that he was delighted with the new technique. We progressed at about 15 mph and soon had two CR42s [Italian biplane fighter aircraft] on fire. As the third one burst into flames I saw Paddy [Mayne] jump out of the leading jeep, run across and throw a Lewes bomb into a cockpit. He just could not resist the temptation of doing things in the old way.'

The raid was a stunning success and resulted in the destruction of nearly 40 enemy aircraft. The SAS's long association with light military vehicles had begun.

As the campaign in North Africa came to an end in May 1943, the SAS (numbering two regiments and a total of around 600 men) faced an uncertain future. However, David Stirling (who had been captured in January 1943) had created an organisation that could fight in all theatres of war, not just the desert. For example, he had insisted that his men be trained to reach their targets by land, sea or air. Thus they were ideally suited to take part in the next phase of Allied strategy: the invasions of Sicily and mainland Italy.

During Operation 'Husky', the invasion of Sicily, the Special Raiding Squadron (1 SAS which had been temporarily renamed) was under the overall control of the British XIII Corps and was tasked with conducting an amphibious assault to capture the enemy gun battery on top of Capo Murro di Porco. The landing was scheduled for 10 July 1943, though the actual assault, like most amphibious operations, was more difficult than expected. Bob Bennett was one of those who took part:

'The sea was roaring away and the ship was heaving from side to side. As each man tried to get into the landing craft, the boats would swing away from the ship, leaving a yawning gap. We eventually got into the craft and headed for the shore. It was about 0200 hours...On the way in, we saw a smashed glider and bodies [Allied soldiers] bobbing up and down in the sea. We couldn't do anything about it, but the bosun returned and picked them up.'

The SAS encountered a new form of combat during this campaign: fighting in built-up areas. Once again, however, the exhaustive training paid dividends. The SAS approached the tasks with a cool professionalism. Bob Bennett describes the clearing of Augusta:

'You just went down both sides of the street with each group covering the buildings on the opposite side. Of course, you had the 'Back Charlie' of each section walking backwards to cover the rear. When we found an occupied building, grenades were the weapon. You just threw a few in and then smashed through the door, spraying the room with fire as you went. We killed quite a few this way, and there weren't many prisoners.'

It was a similar story during the bloody operation to take the Italian town of Bagnara on 3 September 1943:

'We used the local vineyards as cover. You were taught to reserve your ammunition, and we never used a grenade, or fired, unless we knew there was going to be something on the other end of it. The Brens and Vickers were the best weapons out there and did quite a lot of damage to the enemy.'

SAS weapons training, even in the early years, has always been extremely thorough. As they would have to operate behind enemy lines, David Stirling was insistent that all his men be familiar with the enemy's weapons. In fact, enemy weapons were favoured by many SAS soldiers. During the Sicilian campaign, for example, Bennett was equipped with a German submachine gun:

'I had a 9mm Schmeisser I'd picked up from a mined German armoured car in the desert. The British Tommy-guns were no use to us because of the weight of the ammo – you just couldn't carry enough. We carried all sorts of equipment. The grenade discharger cup which fitted onto our rifles was very effective.'

The Special Air Service was heavily engaged in the fight to liberate France and the Low Countries in 1944-45, and also took part in the campaign in Germany at the end of the war. The actions in France after the D-Day landings of 6 June 1944 fell into two main categories: to provide small-scale, tactical support for General Bernard Montgomery's 21st Army Group, and to operate behind enemy lines with local *Maquis*

Below: David Stirling (left) and 'Jock' Lewes talk about operational plans in North Africa, 1942.

groups to disrupt enemy logistics. In the four months after D-Day, some 2000 SAS men were dropped behind enemy lines in France and the Low Countries. Operating in uniform from more than 40 bases, they hit enemy vehicles, railway lines and German military personnel.

As ever, the success of individual SAS missions relied on the skills of the individual soldiers involved. One such operation was Operation 'Kipling', which took place between 13 August and 26 September 1944 in the area west of Auxerre, central France. Captain Derrick Harrison was a member of the SAS team, and he provides an interesting insight into the way SAS soldiers fought behind the lines in France. Both men and jeeps were parachuted into the area by the RAF and, once a base had been established, the jeeps ranged far and wide searching for enemy forces. In one incident on 23 August Harrison, with two jeeps, decided to investigate why smoke was rising into the air from the

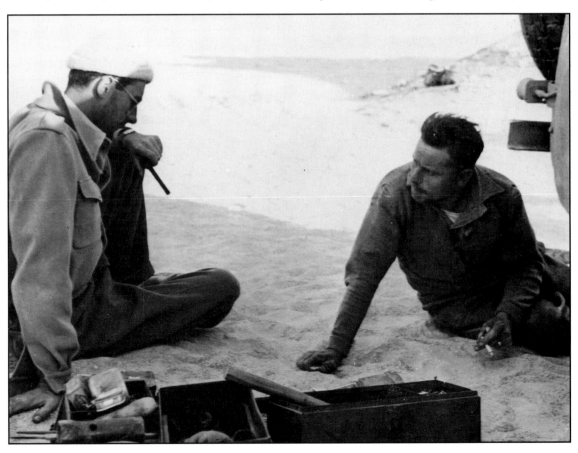

village of Les Ormes. When they got nearer they were informed by a fleeing civilian that the Germans were shooting up the entire village. Harrison's subsequent actions are typical of the quick reactions possessed by SAS soldiers:

'In such situations plans are made at great speed, but they are, nonetheless, plans... Our only hope was a surprise attack: drive through the village at speed and trust to our firepower. The Union Jacks on our jeeps jerked into life as we accelerated into the village square. In the road stood a large German truck and two staff cars, blocking the way through. A crowd of SS men in front of the church dashed for cover as I opened up with my machine guns, and as the vehicles burst into flames, I saw some of the Germans fall. But now I was in trouble. My jeep had come to a sudden halt, my Vickers jammed and the Germans were firing back [the other jeep was in the square, a short distance behind Harrison's].'

Many men in such circumstances would have made a run for it or surrendered. However, Harrison, displaying that typical SAS knack for coolly assessing the situation, decided on another course:

Below: A different theatre: an SAS soldier liaises with partisans in Italy, 1943. The Regiment fought in Italy up until the end of the war.

Above: SAS paratroopers in the fuselage of a Beverley aircraft during the Malayan campaign.

'I had grabbed my carbine and was now standing in the middle of the road firing at everything that moved. Germans seemed to be firing from every doorway. I felt my reactions speed up to an incredible level. It was almost as if I could see individual bullets coming towards me as I ducked and weaved to avoid them. And all the time I was shooting from the hip, and shooting accurately.

'Suddenly, my right hand was warm, wet and with slippery blood. I had been hit. This posed another difficulty: how to change magazines. Somehow, in a fumbling manner, I managed...I moved to the left and saw some 20 men moving through the small walled orchard towards me. Fire! Change mag. Fire! Slowly they fell back, leaving some of their number dead or wounded.'

Harrison managed to reach the other jeep, which made a speedy retreat from the village, leaving some 60 Germans dead and wounded, together with one truck and the two staff cars destroyed. For his bravery that day, Harrison deservedly won the Military Cross. His actions

Above: A four-man patrol takes a breather while on a deep reconnaissance mission in Malaya.

also illustrate that other quality found in SAS soldiers: the ability to keep thinking even when the situation is desperate. This has saved the lives of many SAS men who have been in a tight spot.

The SAS crossed into Germany in the early months of 1945. They took part in many reconnaissance operations and were closely tied to regular formations. Rather than being engaged in deep-penetration hit-and-run raids, the SAS formations were for the most part employed just ahead of the advancing Allied formations. As such they were often subjected to ambushes, which made losses disproportionately high, and the general hostility of the population made operating behind the lines difficult. The jeeps being used by the SAS at this time had been further modified: the whole of the front was covered in armoured plate, there were semi-circles of bullet-proof glass to protect the driver and front gunner, and some were fitted with a wire-cutting device above the front bumper. The

SAS obsession with keeping all equipment in first-class condition was always in evidence. Bob Bennett, the veteran of North Africa, was with D Squadron, 1 SAS, at this time:

'The jeeps always came first. Whenever we halted for the night, each crew checked the tyres, gave the engine the once over and sorted out any faults. Everyone was mechanically minded and many men had been with jeeps since the desert days.'

The balance sheet for the SAS at the end of the campaign in northwest Europe was very favourable: nearly 8000 enemy soldiers killed or wounded, 4784 captured, over 700 vehicles destroyed, including seven trains (an additional 33 trains had been derailed) and 164 railway lines cut. However, with peace came rapid demobilisation, and the Special Air Service was officially disbanded.

It took a conflict in the Far East to provide the impetus to recreate the Regiment. The

Malayan 'Emergency', which began in June 1948, was to result in the reformation of the Special Air Service and the further refinement of its wartime role. The conflict between the British administration in Malaya and the mainly Chinese Malayan Races Liberation Army (MRLA) was to last 12 years, but ultimately the British defeated the Communist Terrorists (CTs), not least due to the efforts of one man and his unit.

Lieutenant-Colonel 'Mad' Mike Calvert was, in many ways, cast in the same mould as David Stirling: he was a man of vision who looked to unconventional ways to solve problems. He was a veteran of the Chindit campaigns in Burma during World War II and had ended the war in Europe as commander of the SAS Brigade. After the initial successes against the CTs in Malaya, the latter had withdrawn deeper into the jungle, from where they launched attacks against British targets. It soon became apparent that the authorities needed a deep-penetration unit to locate and destroy the CT bases.

General Sir John Harding, Commander-in-Chief Far East Land Forces, commissioned Calvert to write a report on all aspects of the war in Malaya. Following six months of research, which involved working with police and Army units and conducting lone reconnaissances in the jungle, he submitted his report. In it he described how he would set up a specialist counter-insurgency force which could live, move and fight the guerrillas in the jungle.

In 1950, in response to the report, Harding authorised Calvert to form the Malayan Scouts. His three- and four-man patrols began to operate effectively against the CTs, laying ambushes, gathering intelligence and establishing contacts with the Aborigines (the original inhabitants who had been forced into the interior by successive waves of invaders). The Scouts, after initial problems, became very successful and this led to the reformation of 22 SAS in 1952. In addition, Calvert believed one of the keys to victory lay in winning over the indigenous Aborigines. This was the beginning of the famous 'hearts and minds' policy that was used in subsequent campaigns.

What was it like fighting in the Malayan jungle? Johnny Cooper, an SAS veteran of World War II, gives a vivid account:

'In areas of dense bamboo we had to do a lot of cutting with our machetes and didn't move very quickly. Worse, the noise we made carried for miles if it wasn't masked by the screams of monkeys. When we moved through swamps, the noise was terrible and, covered in leeches, we were lucky to cover 200yds in an hour.

'Moving through primary jungle was much easier as there was little ground vegetation, but we had to watch out for snakes. We tried to avoid well-used tracks as the CTs often set up ambushes or pig traps of sharpened bamboo along the way.'

Jungle fighting required nerves of steel, endless patience and great reserves of physical stamina. Life on operations was invariably grim: clothes could be soaked with rain or sweat, the environment was mostly dark and damp below the jungle canopy, and there was the ever-present threat of booby traps or an enemy ambush. In addition, there was always the possibility of stumbling on the local wildlife: elephants, tigers, snakes, water buffalo (which could be very hostile), hornets and mosquitoes. Despite this, Cooper for one did not find the jungle itself intimidating:

'I never had a feeling of claustrophobia in the jungle. It was intensely quiet and very cool, and in the more mountainous states in Malaya we would come across many rivers and fast-flowing streams. Carrying up to 60lbs in a bergen plus personal weapons limited the length of time between halts on a patrol. The only Malayan landscape which was a real nightmare were the swampy areas, notably in Selangor. Before my initiation there, I found it hard to believe that it could take up to one hour to cover five hundred yards. The mangrove trees were not particularly tall, so the sun did penetrate, and the water level could be anything up to three feet in depth. The idea was to go from tree to tree stepping on the roots, but every so often you would find yourself up to the waist in gooey black mud. Pulling oneself out with a heavy rucksack on the back was no easy task. In the swamps we also made the acquaintance of the tiger leech which not only sucked blood but hurt as well.'

As the men of the SAS gained skill in the methods of jungle warfare, new tactics were tried in an effort to trap the elusive foe. One of these innovations was 'tree jumping', a parachute technique pioneered by the SAS. As CT camps were located deep in the jungle, it took foot patrols a long time to reach them, giving the enemy the opportunity of escaping. Therefore, the decision was taken to drop men by parachute onto the thick jungle canopy and from there they would use ropes to descend to the ground. The first operational jump was carried out by 54 men in February 1952 near the Thai border. Their role was to act as a blocking force in an operation involving Gurkhas, Royal Marines, Malay Police and more SAS soldiers on the ground. None of the men deployed by parachute were hurt and so the tactic was judged a great success. In fact parachuting into thick trees was a highly dangerous tactic, which was confirmed during subsequent operations when there were many injuries. During Operation 'Sword' in January 1954, for example, three SAS soldiers died when they crashed into the jungle canopy.

By 1958 the conflict in Malaya had almost been won, and the SAS had played a significant part in the victory. In the jungle it had won the hearts and minds of the Aborigines and had made the jungle an unsafe place for the enemy. Both the Malayan Scouts and the SAS proved that British soldiers, so long as they possessed the right qualities and were adequately trained, could operate in the jungle for long periods and take the fight to the opposition. Indeed, many SAS troopers became legendary jungle fighters. And Sergeant Bob Turnbull, a Yorkshireman, became an expert linguist and tracker.

It has always been the proud boast of the SAS that its men, because of their exhaustive training, can fight in any terrain at a moment's notice. In 1958 the SAS was mostly a collection of jungle warriors, but an incident in the Middle East led to the Regiment once again fighting in

the searing heat of the desert. The British government, because it had treaty obligations to the Sultan of Muscat and Oman, found itself being dragged into a counter-insurgency campaign there in the 1950s.

The autocratic rule of the Sultan was being challenged by rebels led by Sulaiman bin Himyar, Ghalib bin Ali and Ghalib's brother, Talib. Armed insurgents had occupied the Jebel Akhdar (meaning 'Green Mountain') in the north of the country in 1957 and declared it independent of the Sultan. The latter called on the British for help, and they despatched an infantry brigade, which restored the Sultan's authority around the Jebel. However, the rebels were still secure on the mountain plateau itself, which covered an area of 350 square kilometres and was surrounded by high peaks. Access to their positions was via narrow passes which could be easily defended. Sooner or later, the British and royalist forces would have to storm the position, a formidable, and potentially bloody, proposition to say the least.

It was inevitable, perhaps, that the Special Air Service should be selected to act as the vanguard. The 70 men of D Squadron arrived in Oman in November 1958 and began operations straight away, establishing positions on the northern side of the Jebel. Several weeks before they had left Malaya, the SAS soldiers undertook training exercises for the new type of terrain they would be operating in, as a corporal of the squadron relates:

> 'Everything was done in the heat of the day. We set up a series of hard marches with bergens, weapons and ammunition, and at the end of each march there was more and more range work, more and more open work, as opposed to work which we'd always done in jungle, and longer range marksmanship, well over the 25 or 30yds which we had previously engaged in.'

The terrain was extremely inhospitable, and was entirely different from that encountered in Malaya. In addition, the rebels were excellent shots and this, combined with the lack of cover,

Above: A motley crew: 16 Troop, D Squadron, 22 SAS, just before the Jebel Akhdar operation.

made movement during daylight difficult. An indication of the type of conditions and enemy the SAS was up against is given by a trooper from D Squadron:

'We got to the top and we found positions that the enemy had obviously occupied, so we decided to get into their positions rather than make new ones of our own, because we knew enough about them to realise that they would spot a new position on the skyline the same as we would if it was our area. At about 0630 the sun came up and we fried and fried and fried. We had two extremes. At night it was cold enough on top of the mountain to freeze the water bottle, and we weren't as well equipped then as we are today. All we had were OG [olive-green] trousers and jackets and a very thin standard issue pullover. We didn't take sleeping-bags on a 24-hour recce since all they did was slow you down, and anyway, we didn't intend to sleep, not

knowing whether they had established night piquets.

'Around about 1400 hours I had another three men with me in my patrol and we were looking down and covering an area when, lo and behold, I saw this Arab start making his way up. He got up to within 300yds of us when he must have spotted some sort of movement because he shouted up at me, obviously thinking I was one of them. So we shouted down, but then he decided, having had his rifle on his shoulder in the sling position, that something wasn't quite right here, so he took it off, whereupon I shot him. My mate alongside me shot him as well and we just blew him away. Within 30 seconds we were under fire from numerous places. They were hyperactive and their reaction was perfect. They started shooting from all areas and concentrating fire on us. Further along the ridge, the other half of our troop was trapped and one of them, Corporal 'Duke' Swindells, was shot.'

Aggressive and bold leadership has always been the hallmark of SAS soldiers, and it was no exception on the Jebel Akhdar. One such officer, who would later achieve fame as the commander of British forces during the 1991 Gulf War against Iraq, was Captain Peter de la Billière. A machine gunner from D Squadron remembers one particular action that de la Billière was involved in:

'As de la Billière's troop had done the recce, they would do the nearest bit and would put a 66mm rocket or Carl Gustav rocket into the [rebel] cave – several in fact. Our troop was designed to cover them and we were on a slightly higher ridge about two or three hundred yards above them. We climbed up that night, early morning came and I was behind the Browning. I had persuaded John Watts that the ideal weapon for Oman was the .30 Browning where you had the range you didn't have with the LMG [light machine gun], but, like all machine guns, it attracts a lot of attention. We set the gun up overlooking the cave and then, first thing in the morning, several men came to the entrance of the cave and were about to start leading the donkeys out. Whereupon, three rounds rapid from the Carl Gustav went straight in the middle and whoof, they blew the cave in and a fair number of them to pieces. Once again, within a minute and a half, we were all under attack. They were amazing in their reactions plus their knowledge of the ground. They were born for it and their reactions were fast. We were under attack from their mortars. We were under attack from their LMGs and from individual tribesmen who were all spoiling for a fight. But, with the help of my machine gun and the RAF who arrived, we extracted ourselves without loss.'

In January 1959 the decision was taken to make a determined push against the rebels. The newly arrived A Squadron under Major Johnny Cooper was tasked with assaulting the enemy from the north while D Squadron attacked from the south. The attack went in at 0300 hours on 26 January. The key to the assault was a strenuous climb running from the village of Kamah up between the Wadi Kamah and the Wadi Suwaiq. A lie had been spread among the Arab donkey handlers that the main attack would come from the direction of Tanuf. This information quickly reached the rebels, who prepared to meet the SAS in the heights above Tanuf. The first attack, however, came from the north, led by Major Cooper:

'I attacked Aquabat al Dhafar with three troops while one, with all the machine guns from the others, laid a barrage on Sabrina [the top of the mountain]. Tony Jeapes' troop was the one that scaled the pinnacle on the high side and got over the top and killed three or four. When Tony got on the top and scarpered these boys, he poured fire down on the other side and won the firefight...By morning my three troops had Sabrina, and the enemy retreated.'

The attack on Sabrina persuaded the rebels to send reinforcements from the village of Saiq to blunt Cooper's attack. Meanwhile, A Squadron left Sabrina and headed down to Tanuf to join D Squadron for the final push.

By 1800 hours on 26 January, A Squadron was in Tanuf and resting, and then both squadrons were loaded into trucks and transported to the assembly area at Kamah. At the same time, a diversionary attack was launched by the SAS up the Wadi Tanuf by a single troop. From Kamah the two squadrons, heavily loaded down with kit, began their ascent. The ruse had been so successful that the men encountered little opposition, though as Cooper remarked of the climb, 'it was bloody difficult and we were carrying a hell of a lot of weight.' Following the SAS were more British troops and contingents of the Sultan's Armed Forces.

Taken by surprise, rebel resistance soon crumbled. The SAS had reached the plateau and were mopping up all opposition. The enemy leaders fled to Saudi Arabia and their men were disarmed. It was a classic SAS operation, and is neatly summed up by Johnny Cooper himself:

'It had to be done quickly. If you'd sent in a battalion of infantry it would have cost a lot of money. Here you were sending only a small gang. It was an SAS job because we had the ability to carry pack-mule loads and we were all very fit.'

In fact, the Jebel Akhdar operation was a supreme example of how a small, specialist force, if led correctly, can achieve results out of all proportion to its size. The SAS mission did not end with the assault on the Jebel. The men then began an immediate 'hearts and minds' campaign to turn the local inhabitants into supporters of the Sultan.

The next SAS operation was to see the Regiment return to the jungles of the Far East, specifically Borneo. By this time SAS drills and procedures had been amended and refined since the days in North Africa during World War II. For example, the Regiment's soldiers were learning how to operate with helicopters, and jungle warfare techniques had been perfected in the jungles of Malaya. However, one thing that hadn't changed was the calibre of recruits accepted into the Regiment. If anything, the entry requirements were higher than ever. By 1960 the Regiment had its own base in the UK and, thanks to the earlier efforts of Lieutenant-Colonel John Woodhouse, it had an excellent Selection Training programme that quickly weeded out those who were unsuitable material. The British Special Air Service was now truly one of the world's elite units.

Below: A photograph that conveys the conditions encountered by SAS soldiers on the Jebel Akhdar.

BORNEO

Militarily, the jungle can be a potential disaster area, but in the early 1960s the SAS fought a highly effective jungle campaign in Borneo, and, in a series of top-secret cross-border raids, struck a number of decisive blows against the Indonesian Army.

The jungle in Borneo is of two main types: primary jungle and secondary jungle. The former contains trees that can grow up to a height of over 60m, forming a thick canopy of leaves that ensures very little light reaches the jungle floor. This means visibility can be reduced to 50m or less, though a bonus is that there is little undergrowth to hinder movement. Secondary jungle occurs where sunlight reaches the jungle floor, such as around river banks and where primary jungle has been cleared. In this type of terrain the ground is covered by grasses, ferns and shrubs. Movement is slow and can be very tiring, with many hours spent hacking a path with machetes (this is invariably very noisy and will therefore alert an enemy of a patrol's presence – something an SAS unit will wish to avoid).

Everyone sweats in the jungle (Borneo was unlike the cool, mountainous regions encountered by Johnny Cooper in Malaya), but soldiers carrying heavy loads will perspire a lot more. In addition, disease and parasites thrive in a jungle environment, thus soldiers need to be on their guard against infection. What qualities are needed to fight in the jungle?

A patrol moves along a river in Borneo. Fighting in such terrain can be an absolute nightmare, as the humidity is oppressive, and soldiers have to be on constant guard against ambush.

First and foremost is physical fitness. Wading through a swamp for hours on end, for example, carrying a weapon over your head, is a severe test of fitness. To achieve the required level of fitness the Americans believe a soldier should go into the jungle 'lean and mean' to fight. But the SAS takes a different view: it encourages its soldiers to go into the jungle overweight because they will invariably lose a lot of weight and come out 'lean and mean'. Mental preparedness is also important. The jungle is dark, dank and can be claustrophobic. Soldiers need to be 'switched on' to operate effectively, otherwise lethargy and apathy can quickly set in. A veteran of A Squadron describes his first contact with the jungle:

> 'The humidity of the jungle is not immediately obvious because the canopy of trees casts a psychological shadow of coolness. So you think, well, this isn't so bad after all. But then the humidity hits you, and within an hour both your trousers and shirt are saturated with sweat as the body soaks up the rising warmth. The best way I can describe it is being inside a greenhouse which has no lights. The sun can be scorching the tops of the trees, but on the ground the atmosphere is constantly damp.'

Wearing the right gear is also very important: one of the most important items of clothing is footwear. The feet and legs must be protected at all times. Contrary to popular opinion, most animals – snakes, wild pigs and large mammals – will move away from people who are moving through the jungle. However, there is still a risk of walking into a scorpion or spider's nest, and if this happens and you're not wearing tough boots, the consequences can be dire. However, the standard British Army issue items were not always up to the required standard:

> 'Canvas boots to allow the feet to sweat were issued, but early designs suffered due to the poor quality of the material. Some blokes used their initiative and got cobblers in Singapore, who could make you a pair of shoes in an hour, to stitch a piece of soft leather to their DMS (Direct Moulded Sole) boots. Others had bartered to acquire the more professional-looking US and Australian jungle boots, which had a hard rubber sole with breathable strong uppers.'

The head was also protected, though the SAS had to tailor the issue item to its own needs:

> 'Whoever designed the standard British Army "bush" hat had obviously never been in the jungle. It was probably great for keeping the sun off on Brighton beach, but it was useless in the *ulu* (jungle). The brim was so big that it actually blocked out what little light the jungle offered, and when moving through dense areas of jungle it often caught on branches. To solve the problem we employed the standard regimental answer to problems: cut it off.'

Likewise with the legs and arms: they must be protected at all times from bites and scratches:

> 'Anyone who went into the jungle with a short-sleeved shirt was asking for trouble. Shirt sleeves were always rolled down to stop insects from clinging to you and to prevent your arms coming into contact with foliage, the sap of which could give you a nasty rash.'

Ironically, animals could also pose a danger to the patrol as they ran away from the troops who were moving through the jungle:

> 'The *ulu*, the name we called the jungle, is alive with a background noise of wildlife, which increases to a thunderous roar at dawn and last light. However, great care is needed when moving because the animals can sense your approach and disappear, leaving a silence which can compromise your position to an alert enemy.'

This, then, was the type of terrain and the conditions SAS soldiers found themselves

Above: Royal Marines move along a river in the Sabah region of Borneo, 1965. Boats were a quick way to travel, but were vulnerable to ambushes.

campaigning in during the 1960s in Borneo. What was the background to the conflict? Malaya, the former British colony, was pushing hard in the early 1960s for the formation of a new political entity in the region, to comprise Sabah, Sarawak, Brunei, Malaya and Singapore (on the Malay Peninsula), and which would be called the Federation of Malaysia. The general idea was supported by Britain but was violently opposed by President Sukarno of Indonesia, who saw the scheme as a hindrance to Indonesia's expansionist aims. The bulk of the island of Borneo was actually part of Indonesia, and was known as Kalimantan.

In early 1963 Sukarno began the infiltration of insurgents from Kalimantan into Sarawak and Sabah, a process that was speeded up when Sabah and Sarawak were officially incorporated into Malaysia in September 1963. The British responded to this action, forming a force of Malaysian, British and Commonwealth troops to fight the insurgents. Part of this effort was the Special Air Service. Not that the British had an easy task: Major-General Walter Walker, the Director of Operations Borneo, had only five

battalions to cover some 1500km of jungle-covered, often unexplored, border. He also had to contend with an internal threat in the shape of the Clandestine Communist Organisation (CCO), whose recruits came predominantly from the Chinese settlers in Sarawak.

The first SAS unit to arrive in Borneo, in early 1963, was A Squadron, 22 SAS, and the Regiment's commander, Lieutenant-Colonel John Woodhouse. Walker originally wanted to use the SAS as a kind of mobile reserve, dropped by parachute onto the jungle canopy in order to recapture areas captured by the Indonesians. Woodhouse, convinced this tactic would result in high casualties, persuaded him that the SAS would be better suited to operating in small patrols along the border, where they could gather timely intelligence concerning enemy incursions. Though it numbered only 70 men, by operating in two- or three-man patrols the squadron was able to field 21 patrols along the entire length of the border. They also stayed in the jungle for long periods: one patrol stayed in the Long Jawi area for six months.

Contact with the local inhabitants formed an important part of SAS operations and a 'hearts and minds' policy (see Chapter 2) was quickly implemented. The procedure was for the patrol to establish contact with the local inhabitants and gain their trust. Often the SAS soldiers would live with the locals, sharing their longhouses and helping with the planting and harvesting of crops. In this way, over time, trust was built up between the natives and the SAS soldiers. The man most responsible for winning over these people, however, was the patrol medic. The work he did in curing their ills reaped substantial rewards when it came to gathering intelligence concerning enemy strengths and dispositions. But that was later in the campaign. The first SAS deployment, at the end of 1962, was to Brunei:

> 'The Regiment had served in the Malayan conflict, so we were fairly well qualified for jungle operations. President Sukarno, nicknamed "the mad doctor", was doing everything in his power to unite the whole area under his leadership. Some rebels tried to foment trouble in Brunei, but this was quickly suppressed by British forces (though not SAS). We flew into Singapore, where we were briefed by a Gurkha major concerning the situation in Borneo. Several battalions, which had been serving in Singapore, were subsequently deployed to Sarawak, including 650 Gurkhas.'

Once in Borneo the SAS was tasked with gathering intelligence. The Regiment also trained a number of irregular forces, known as Border Scouts, as aids to intelligence gathering. They were created by Major-General Walker as part of an effort to establish a defensive intelligence network, along the border with Kalimantan. The Scouts were recruited from the indigenous tribes of the region and were trained by SAS soldiers in a number of camps. Armed and trained as paramilitaries, the Border Scouts were not combat troops. Their task was to move

through the jungle unseen and gather valuable information. When they did engage Indonesian forces the consequences were often dire: in September 1963, for example, a Border Scout post at Long Jawi, 45km from the border, was wiped out by a large party of Indonesian troops. But in the intelligence-gathering role the Scouts could be invaluable for acting as the 'eyes and ears' along the border, and individual Scouts were often attached to SAS patrols to aid communications with the indigenous tribes in the area where the soldiers were operating. During the initial stages of the campaign the SAS's role was straightforward:

> 'Our role was very simple, ie to go into the jungle and gather information about the Indos and their tactics. We did this by befriending the local tribes and lying up in a deep-camouflaged "hide" [covert position] on the border to monitor activity. We didn't initially mount fighting patrols, whose sole purpose was to go and engage the enemy, but in the course of this intelligence work we did occasionally get bumped by an Indo ambush. We also sprang one ourselves from time to time.'

The SAS patrols also established ambush sites for other units and potential helicopter landing zones. Any intelligence that was collected was relayed back to SAS headquarters by high-frequency radio, where it could be acted upon immediately. The Indonesian incursions into Sarawak began in April 1963, by which time A Squadron had an effective 'hearts and minds' policy up and running. The unit was relieved by D Squadron in May 1963, and the SAS began to pay attention to likely Indonesian infiltration points: the tracks leading through Stass at Long Jawi, the plains along parts of Sarawak's western frontier, the valleys south of Pensiangan, and the estuaries of eastern Sabah and Kalabakan. During this time the squadron also undertook a reconnaissance of the previously unexplored area in southern Sabah known as 'The Gap'.

Despite the British effort, Indonesian incursions increased steadily during the winter of 1963-64, especially along the borders of Sabah and Sarawak. SAS personnel, because of their knowledge of the terrain and the relationships they had established with the indigenous tribes, began to assist regular infantrymen in stopping infiltrations by escorting them to ambush sites. The increasing number of Indonesian incursions meant SAS patrols encountered the enemy more often. A trooper from D Squadron relates of one such contact:

'In late 1964 our four-man patrol was heading back to base camp after six days in the *ulu*. The plan was to get back before last light, but the mountainous countryside and the Indos had other ideas. A rope toggle is standard equipment in the jungle. It is about 5m long and is used for crossing fast-flowing rivers or streams by hooking the toggles together. This simple system allows the team to hook up to each other and cross dangerous water with some degree of safety.

'Anyway we reached a section of the river that was narrow but deep. We were armed with Armalites [M16s]. When the Regiment first arrived in Borneo the SLR was standard issue, but within a short space of time the American Armalite was introduced. Though it doesn't have long range, it is light and compact, and is ideally suited to jungle warfare. We scanned the opposite bank for any signs of an enemy presence. So far, so good. Then, as I prepared to cross over, I saw a black flash on the other side. Before I could react the river bank was being riddled with machine-gun fire, quickly followed by frenzied bursts from the Armalites. Our

Below: Effecting a river crossing in Borneo, which invariably results in being covered in leeches.

Iban scout [native inhabitant of Sarawak] had earlier warned us that something was wrong. They were amazing those little guys, they could see and hear things that we would never perceive. I was bloody glad we had them, I can tell you. Anyway, our scout had dived behind this boulder as the GPMG and Armalites put a hail of shot into the space where we had seen the

hostile. The Indo didn't have a chance, he went down in an instant.

'The contact was over in seconds and the jungle fell silent. We had killed one Indonesian but there might be more nearby. By this time I had taken cover and, like everyone else, scanned the area for signs of any more of the opposition. Then we quickly bugged out and moved

Left: An SAS patrol rests while on a cross-border raid. Note the M16 in the bottom left-hand corner.

the Indo's head and stuffed it into his bag! "Good money, good money," he kept repeating, referring to the bounty he would receive from the Brunei government.

'Ibans were natural trackers and several patrols developed a strong rapport with their own man. Ours would always carry an old pack he had acquired from an infantry battalion. It was full of what appeared to be tree bark and animal skin, which he often chewed on, giving his teeth a tobacco-stained look. They were great blokes, though their headhunting habits were a little disconcerting. We had to continually remind ourselves that it was part of their culture and had been going on for years. It was naturally encouraged by the Brunei government, who wanted as many Indonesian soldiers dead as possible, hence the bounty. The Ibans then suddenly stopped acquiring heads and started to collect ears (the heads were taking up too much space in their bergens!). Mind you, their habits stopped anyone going into their backpacks!'

SAS soldiers received thorough training before being sent to fight in the jungle. All the Regiment's men were taught the basics of jungle survival skills, such as finding food and water, constructing shelters, working with primitive medicines and jungle navigation:

'Specialist training for this type of warfare is essential. Without good jungle knowledge you can easily fall victim to the terrain and its hostile environment. If you don't know how to operate in the tropics you can end up being killed.'

Specialised training and state-of-the-art equipment often go hand in hand, and the popular image of the Special Air Service is of a body of men kitted out with the very best that money can buy. Though this might be true now,

downstream, taking up defensive positions and waiting for the Indos to mount a follow-up ambush. However, they didn't bother and we speedily crossed the river. There is one interesting postscript to the story. Our tracker, who spoke English, said he would check the body. Before we knew what he was up to, he came running back with a big smile on his face. He had cut off

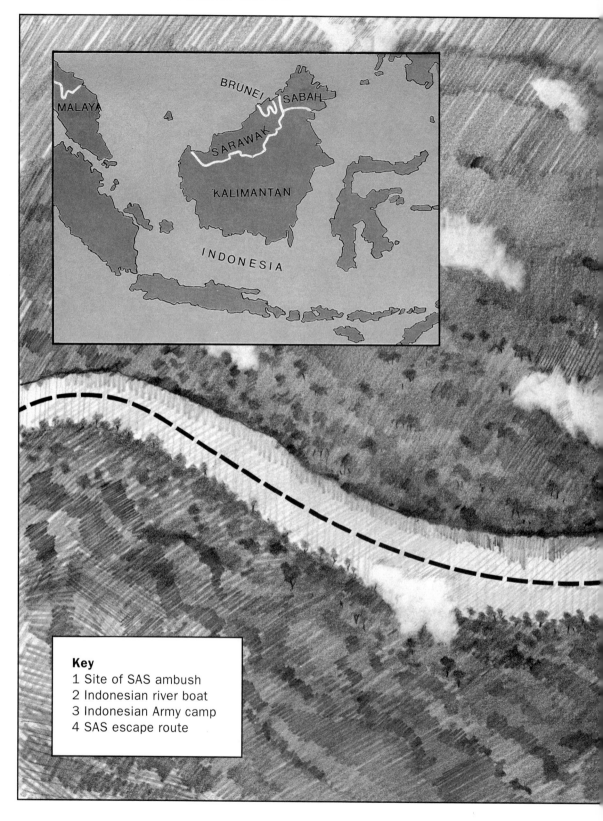

Key
1 Site of SAS ambush
2 Indonesian river boat
3 Indonesian Army camp
4 SAS escape route

in Borneo this certainly wasn't the case, as this ex-trooper from A Squadron relates:

'At that time we carried 'A-frame' bergens – so called because of the arrangement of the metal bars that held the bergen – and a motley collection of webbing pouches that were hijacked from various sources. The pouches always held our top priorities: ammunition and survival kits. In the main we used the '44-pattern webbing which has top fasteners to allow easy access to the water pouch. We usually combined these with bits of Aussie kit. A '58-pattern yoke was added to this customised system to take the weight from the hips to the shoulders. The webbing was held together by a quick-release belt which had been adapted from RAF heavy-load straps, thus we could jettison the kit quickly if we had to run like fuck after being bumped. However, the overriding factor was that every piece of kit could be easily fitted onto any set of webbing carried by other members of the team if the need arose. The thing was, in the early 1960s the Regiment was reduced in strength and we didn't have the priority for equipment that other units had. As a result, we sometimes looked like a bunch of military misfits, having begged, borrowed and stolen a lot of our personal equipment.'

At the beginning of the Borneo campaign the Regiment had only two squadrons, but this soon changed when it became clear the SAS was achieving excellent results. B Squadron was reformed in January 1964, and in 1966 a fourth squadron, G Squadron, was formed from guardsmen who had been conducting SAS-type operations with the Guards Independent Parachute Company in Sarawak.

Despite the increase in numbers, the SAS role remained the same: intelligence gathering. This was made more difficult by the fact that the enemy was not a bunch of ill-armed bandits:

'Of course we got involved in ambushes and firefights, but the image of the SAS charging through the *ulu* with guns blazing at ill-equipped Indos couldn't be further from the truth. The Indos were well armed and organised. It wasn't a situation where you could launch a battalion offensive to crush the guerrillas in one clean swoop. The terrain didn't allow it and neither did the enemy. They had a big advantage in that they knew the terrain, its dangers and, like us, had recruited tribesmen as informants to supply their chain of intelligence with hard-core information. The only way forward for us was to play the same game.'

Though the idea of administering medical aid to native men and women is perhaps contrary to the media image of the SAS, the 'hearts and minds' policy was the key to winning the intelligence war. The concept had been devised by the Military Commissioner in Malaya, General Sir Gerald Templar, to defeat communist insurgents there in the 1950s. It concentrated on gaining the trust of the local inhabitants by learning their language, customs and sharing their lifestyle, and thus winning them over. An SAS trooper describes the standard procedure:

'The four-man patrol would first monitor the village – it wasn't a case of just walking in and saying hello. A lot of these people were very nervous about meeting whites, especially if the Indos had stirred them up. In any case, we always remembered that headhunting was one of their pastimes. When it was deemed safe to enter we did so and attempted to strike up a conversation with the headman. We also offered minor gifts, mainly from our ration packs, to the children. Usually the meeting would go fairly well. If it did we would then leave the village, to return a few days later. You've got to be patient with these people.

'The make-up of an SAS four-man patrol is a medic, a signaller, an explosives expert and a linguist. In Borneo our medics soon became expert "bush doctors", setting up surgery amidst

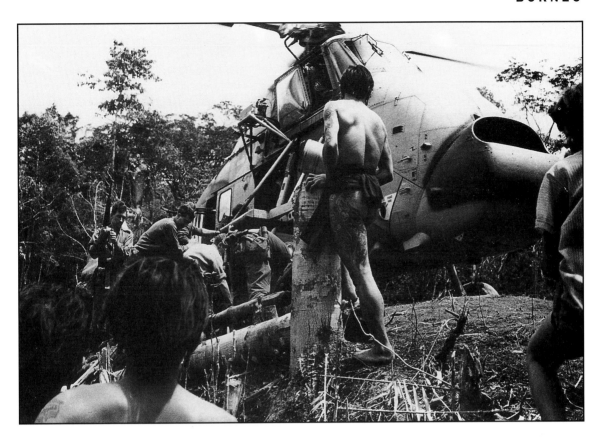

Above: An SAS team is evacuated by a Wessex helicopter after an operation. SAS patrols also guided heliborne troops to ambush locations.

villagers whose ailments would shock the most hardened NHS doctors. These one-man field hospitals were a great success. The improvement in health of those treated boosted confidence and resulted in many patrols being invited to eat with the local community. It was invaluable in winning over the locals, and allowed us to collate vital intelligence about the Indos which we could use to break their supply routes. The locals also gave us bits of information, which were useful in building up an overall picture in the area we were operating in.'

Life on operations didn't just involve living with the natives. Many SAS patrols established observation posts deep in the jungle. Working in covert 'hides' is never easy, but in the jungle SAS soldiers encountered fresh difficulties:

'All year round the dense undergrowth of the jungle hides a host of potential hazards that can drive you mad if you are sat rigid

in a jungle "hide" trying desperately not to make any noise as you monitor the enemy. Red ants, scorpions, leeches, snakes, huge flying beetles and wild pigs head the list. The important thing to remember about all these creatures is that the jungle is their home, and if you leave your kit on the deck they will set up camp inside it. Leaving your boots open to the elements outside your basha is to invite scorpions and small snakes to crawl inside.'

Moving through the jungle, straining to see and hear the slightest sounds that may indicate an enemy presence, soldiers sometimes forget that there are animals around them. A former member of B Squadron tells of a particularly painful experience he had when on patrol near the Indonesian border in late 1964:

'As point man, the leading member of the patrol, I signalled for the team to stop and listen, a common military practice carried out to hear for any sounds of an enemy you can't see because of the undergrowth. As I stood up I was hit several times in the face by what felt like tiny darts. I fell to the ground and quickly discovered I had been stung by a number of hornets. The pain was excruciating and my face quickly swelled to the size of a melon, forcing the patrol to abandon the whole operation. Other teams ran into similar problems with snakes and scorpions.

'In the sticky climate the body is forced to work overtime, and the risk of infection is ever-present. A simple sweat rash caused by not washing, for example, can turn into a health hazard within days, a fact discovered by many of the battalions who served in Borneo. Water is crucial to survival in the jungle. The huge amount of fluid loss meant that each man had to drink at least six bottles of water a day when he first went into the jungle, though this would drop as he became acclimatised to the conditions. As a consequence, each man carried the standard three water bottles and more in his bergen. Essential items of kit were water sterilisation tablets. These killed the tiny water worm that was known to live in the rivers and streams and which could cause a serious stomach upset that could put a trooper out of action for days, even weeks.

'A millbag, used to drain moss, flies and insect debris from still water in areas of deep primary jungle where running water was difficult to find, reduced the risk of contracting leptospirosis, a disease spread via the urine of infected animals, which could be fatal. Malaria was kept at bay by taking paludrine.'

By the winter of 1963-64, because of the substantial rise in enemy activity, it became clear that the British would have to go on to the offensive in order to contain the situation. Therefore, in June 1964 the government authorised Walker to launch the first top-secret 'Claret' raids across the border to pre-empt the build-up of enemy forces in Kalimantan by striking at the opposition's forward bases. The first was launched in June against an Indonesian camp at Nantakor and was entirely successful. The SAS soldiers were usually lightly armed and carried a minimum amount of supplies. They called themselves the 'Tip Toe Boys' because they hit the opposition and then vanished. The Regiment also trained 40 specially selected Border Scouts, known as Cross-Border Scouts, to support its clandestine raids. The Scouts' initial training was supervised by Major John Edwardes of A Squadron, 22 SAS, and their first mission took place in August 1964. Thereafter, they were active along the border, especially in western Sarawak and around Bemban.

An SAS trooper who took part in the 'Claret' operations remembers the procedures for cross-border missions:

'It was impressed upon us that there was to be no evidence left in Kalimantan that British troops had been operating there. Thus casualties, no matter how serious, were always taken back with us, though we could not call in helicopter casualty evacuation. These raids were never officially recorded, but they did give the Regiment the free rein it had been seeking with regard to crossing the border and attacking Indo military targets, which had been identified by our scouts and our own men. A dangerous, though effective, method to hit the enemy's camps was to track an Indo patrol across the border, identify its position, and then call up a "killer" group from an infantry battalion to mount a first-light raid.

'Every SAS patrol was preceded by personal and team checks. We all carried morphine in a metal ampoule around our necks, along with identification disks and a watch. Items of kit such as watch straps were an open invitation to a leech to make itself at home. They always positioned themselves between the strap and your skin, which was extremely irritating. In addition, little things like making sure the buttons on your shirt sleeves had not come off were seemingly unimportant, but they were a barrier to leeches and made the difference between being comfortable and having a thoroughly miserable time. If any man was killed on a "Claret" job he was immediately stripped of any identification and the body buried. We couldn't afford to take any chances.'

Both A and B Squadrons conducted a number of cross-border raids in the second half of 1964. B Squadron was concentrated in the Pueh range of hills in western Sarawak, which was a favourite route for Clandestine Communist Organisation (CCO) agents making their way to Lundu on the coast to foment trouble (the CCO had many cells operating in Sarawak, and the organisation was provided with arms and training bases by President Sukarno). D Squadron replaced A in early 1965 and it also carried out a number of cross-border recce missions. One such operation,

in the Sentimo swamp, resulted in the sinking of an Indonesian river boat by a four-man patrol (see diagram on pages 140-141).

In late May 1965, D Squadron was replaced by A, the latter being commanded by Major Peter de la Billière. In August he launched a series of cross-border raids which kept the pressure on the Indonesians. The standard formation for SAS 'Claret' missions was the four-man patrol:

'Usually the lead man would be armed with a shotgun, the second and third men with Armalites, with the rear man carrying a general purpose machine gun. We experimented with a number of formations, including putting the machine gunner at the front. To make it easier for him we took the butt off and used the gun's sustained fire back plate instead. We also got an armourer to remove the flash

Below: An SAS trooper with captured Indonesians. Captives could be a good source of intelligence.

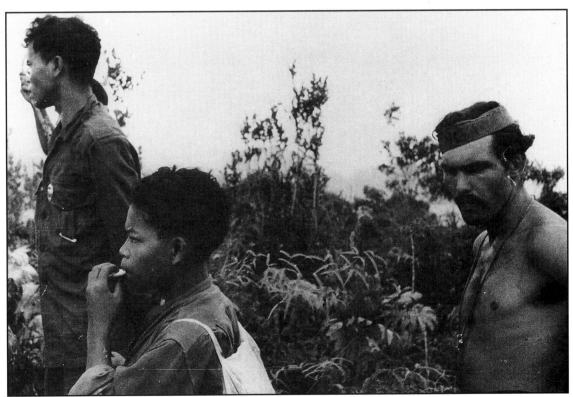

eliminator. The idea was that if we were bumped the point man could open up and spray a burst of wild fire into the bush, which would keep the Indos' heads down and give the rest of the team vital seconds in which to locate the source of the ambush and direct controllable fire at it. Well, that was the theory.

'At first we had a host of problems with the shotgun cartridges. They were paper and they swelled up in the humidity of the jungle. Even carrying them in a plastic bag didn't solve the problem because the bag just filled with condensation. In the end they were replaced by plastic cartridges, which pleased everyone no end.'

Stealth is a major part of SAS operations, but during the cross-border raids the soldiers of the Regiment had to maintain extra vigilance. Even simple procedures presented problems:

'Our bashas, or jungle beds, had to be off the ground to avoid the legions of ants and wild animals that passed by. You can make them easily enough by cutting some wood and building a stretcher and perching it on an A-frame of branches, or constructing a box-type arrangement between a number of trees. However, the

Below: SAS-trained Iban tribesmen bring in Indonesian prisoners following a cross-border raid.

noise created when cutting the wood could be a problem and so we often used a hammock strung between two trees, with a poncho tied overhead to keep the dew and the early morning rain off. After last light we usually got out of our OGs (olive-greens) and put a zoot suit on (a one-piece item of clothing made out of parachute silk which was light and comfortable to sleep in and gave us a chance to dry out our kit).

'Our ration packs, or rat-packs as they were known, consisted of the standard A-, B- and C-type menus and, if you were unlucky, a Gurkha menu, full of curried this and that. Other nutritional delights included meat blocks coated with a disgusting taste of salt.'

Crossing the border was fraught with danger, as the Indonesians were excellent jungle warfare soldiers and they knew their own territory very well. A member of A Squadron describes a cross-border raid into Kalimantan in August 1965:

'When we were across the border we always dismantled our bashas before first light and then moved to a higher position, where we would stop for food and make a call to base camp. At first we made good progress and the journey was uneventful, but then we reached a clearing and we sensed something was wrong. So we sat still for several minutes just listening. Nothing happened. Ten minutes later we got up and moved off, only to walk straight into an Indo ambush. A split second after they opened up we were pouring fire into them. I fired my Armalite from the hip, though in truth it was impossible to see the target and we could only fire at the general area we believed the attack was coming from. In what seemed like a long time, though no doubt it was only a few seconds, we had pulled back and were in cover. We stopped firing, none of the lads had been killed but one had been wounded.

'Next thing I heard what appeared to be a herd of elephants thundering through the bush towards us. It was the Indos coming straight for us to finish the job. Their superior knowledge of the jungle gave them an overwhelming self-confidence. Our Armalites had a hand grip fitted to the stock to give us a better hold, and I tightened my grip as the opposition got nearer. My heart was pounding and I could feel droplets of sweat running down the sides of my face. The first Indo appeared, to be literally cut to pieces by a fusillade of 5.56mm rounds. The look on his face was one of surprise as the bullets tore through his uniform and into his body. He went down. We then hurled grenades into the path of the other Indos, and the whole area was suddenly filled with the choking smell of cordite.

'Then everything was still, with only the lingering smoke from the grenades being a reminder of the act of carnage that had just taken place. I clipped a fresh magazine into my weapon and gingerly edged forward. The other lads did the same. We found the Indos, or what was left of them, a few metres in front of our position. Their eyes were open and a look of pain was etched in their faces. One looked like he was only about 18 years old, which was sad. Then again, he was prepared to kill so it was him or us. After taking details of their unit markings and anything they were carrying that might be useful to the intelligence boys, we legged it. Turned out that the Indos were the remains of a patrol that had been chewed up by a group of Gurkhas on our side of the border. They were heading back to their camp when they came across our patrol.'

The SAS raids continued into 1966, by which time it had become apparent to the Indonesians that Britain would continue to support Malaysia and that the war would not be over quickly. The Indonesian military overthrew President Sukarno in March 1966 and hostilities ceased five months later. The victory was mainly due to the SAS, which had demonstrated what a small number of properly trained and motivated soldiers could do.

THE BATTLE OF MIRBAT

Of all the actions that the SAS has taken part in since its creation, the one that occurred at the small Omani port of Mirbat in July 1972 is perhaps the most famous. It remains an outstanding example of the martial skills of individual SAS soldiers.

What took place at Mirbat is a fine illustration of the weapons skills and overall calibre of SAS soldiers. In addition, it came at a crucial time in the war between the Sultan of Muscat and Oman and the forces of the communist People's Front for the Liberation of the Occupied Arabian Gulf (PFLOAG), and was probably the one event that eventually ensured that the British-backed Sultan achieved victory. But why were British soldiers fighting in Oman in the first place?

Oman as a country has very little going for it, being poor, barren and having an inhospitable climate. This has produced a population which is hardy and extremely poor, whose main support in their lives is an unshakeable belief in Islam. Typically ruled over by autocratic despots, the country resembles a medieval kingdom with twentieth-century trappings. Britain had signed a treaty of friendship with the

SAS troops and *firqat* in Oman during the war against the PFLOAG. Ex-communist guerrillas trained by the SAS, the *firqats* were hardy, if at times infuriating, fighters.

Sultan of Muscat in 1789, giving the East India Company commercial rights in exchange for the protection of the Royal Navy. The treaty was mutually beneficial: Oman was a sea-going nation that had interests in East Africa, Zanzibar, Socotra and Baluchistan, but its interests were threatened by the many pirates who infested the Gulf. The presence of the Royal Navy did much to make the seas a safe place for trade. By the twentieth century the pirates had disappeared, but the British were happy to maintain the ties that had been built up with the various rulers of Oman. And then came along a new factor: oil. Oman is situated on the southeast corner of the Arabian peninsula. This means that it is strategically vital as far as the West's oil supplies are concerned, as a hostile regime could technically halt those supplies.

In the late 1950s the British were called on to support the Sultan, Said bin Taimur, in his efforts to defeat the rebels in the north of his country. Fortunately, the British government had the SAS at its disposal, and two squadrons, supported by some conventional units, did the work of two battalions and defeated the rebels in the famous Jebel Akhdar operation. The country seemingly settled down. However, the policies of Said bin Taimur were repressive to say the least, and in the province of Dhofar, in the southwest of his country, they resulted in the people taking up arms against him in 1962. The Dhofaris formed the Dhofar Liberation Front (DLF), which had as its aims the modernisation of the province and the rather nebulous policy of 'Dhofar for the Dhofaris'. Essentially traditionalist and emphasising the Moslem religion, the DLF's fighters were poorly equipped and trained. In response, the sultan deployed around 1000 men of the Sultan's Armed Forces (SAF) to the area to contain the rebellion. Initially this worked, but to the west, in the Marxist People's Democratic Republic of Yemen (PDRY), storm clouds were gathering.

In the PDRY there was another group, the PFLOAG, which entered the war in Dhofar. The DLF was quickly subsumed into the larger,

more radical group, and soon the scales were tipped against the sultan's forces. In fact, the SAF didn't have the manpower or training to conduct an effective counter-insurgency war. By 1970 the communist PFLOAG, backed by both the Soviet Union and China, had control of the whole of the Jebel Dhofar. Said bin Taimur was staring defeat in the face and the PFLOAG

Right: Soldiers of the Sultan's Armed Forces (SAF). The SAF worked closely with the SAS in Oman.

sensed victory. However, as so often happens in war, events were to take a strange turn.

In July 1970 Said bin Taimur was deposed in a bloodless palace coup by his son, Qaboos, who immediately announced a general amnesty and plans for civil development in Oman. That same month, the first SAS detachments arrived in the country to support the new sultan. They were called British Army Training Teams (shortened to BAT Teams) so the British government, ever the pragmatists, could deny that any of their combat troops were present in Oman. The SAS set about implementing a 'hearts and minds' policy (see Chapter 2), which was aided by the new sultan's measures, and the situation stabilised. But victory was another matter. The SAS received an unexpected boost in its efforts when a number of rebel fighters, alienated by the anti-moslem and hard-line communist ideology of the PFLOAG, surrendered to the Omani government. The leader of the men, Salim Mubarak, advocated turning his men into an anti-rebel group, called a *firqat*. The SAS began training Salim's men, and very soon the first of many *firqats*, the *Firqat Salahadin*, was formed.

By the end of 1971 the Omani government had made substantial gains in Dhofar, with a number of *firqat* groups up and running and the SAS 'hearts and minds' programme working well. The rebels, in response, decided that a victory was needed to persuade the people that their cause would eventually triumph. They decided to mount an attack against the coastal town of Mirbat, some 65km east of Salalah. The following account of the battle is told by a current member of the Regiment, using first-hand accounts told to him by SAS soldiers who fought in Oman in the early 1970s:

'Mirbat. What a god-forsaken place it is. A few mud-built houses clustered around the bay, with some strongpoints located to the north. It was July 1972, the monsoon season was under way and the whole team felt cheesed off. There were nine SAS soldiers in total, including the boss, Captain Mike Kealy. He was only 23 years old and was regarded as being "green". Although most guys in the Regiment have respect for their officers, Kealy was still called a "baby Rupert" by his men. Nevertheless, he was to prove shit-hot when it came to the crunch.

'For three months the SAS soldiers had been at Mirbat as the resident BAT Team, training the *firqats*, or "firqs" as they were called, in the use of infantry weapons. The enemy, the *adoo*, were always in the surrounding hills, but the SAS didn't bother about them too much. They would launch the odd artillery attack on Mirbat which usually fell well short, but apart from that it was pretty quiet. The soldiers had more trouble with the "firqs", who could be real pains in the arse if they

wanted to be. Once they got something into their heads that was it. They called the SAS soldiers "batmen" and believed they came from a special bat regiment, and nothing could alter their opinion.

'Anyway, the training went on and the days ticked by. The weather was miserable (it was the monsoon season): depressing drizzle always hanging over the town and a blanket of low cloud hiding the hills and mountains that surrounded the town.'

The fact that the SAS soldiers could not observe the surrounding hills was a disaster, for in those hills the rebels were assembling a large amount of firepower and men to ensure they would achieve victory. The balance sheet of the opposing forces made grim reading for the SAS men. The rebels numbered around 250 men, all of them seasoned fighters who believed in, and were prepared to die for, their cause. They were armed with a variety of weapons, including Kalashnikov automatic rifles, 75mm recoilless rifles, mortars and Carl Gustav rocket launchers. The SAS soldiers had no idea of what was about to hit them:

'For the most part the SAS men wore cut-down jungle hats, and some of the lads stitched a neck flap to the rear to avoid getting too much sun on the back of their necks, which can cause sunstroke and sickness. Light olive-green trousers and green fatigue shirts were supported by plain green windproof jackets to combat the cold nights. On their feet they wore soft pigskin boots, nicknamed "desert wellies". As always they never went anywhere without their "belt order", which included water, ammunition, survival and escape-and-evasion kits. For weapons they had the SLR and American M16 rifles, plus L42 sniper rifles.

'The men's tour had been uneventful and they were more than ready to be

Right: Have M16, will travel. A member of D Squadron, 22 SAS, in Oman, 1971. The casual appearance belies a trained medic and linguist.

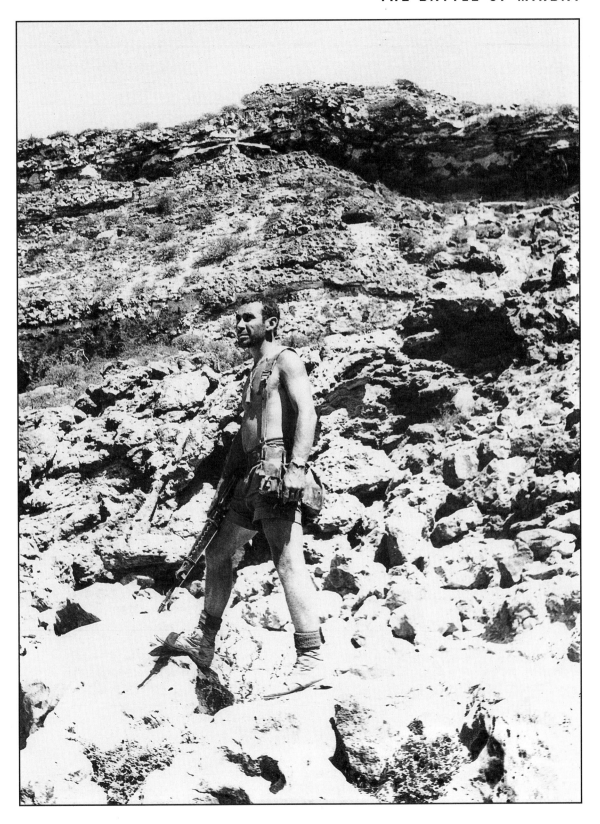

relieved by the next team. The day of departure came through – 19 July – the same day the *adoo* intended to take the town. When people see pictures of the *adoo* they think they were a bunch of ill-armed bandits. Nothing could be further from the truth. Their attack on Mirbat, for example, was well planned. They knew the bad weather would prevent any air cover from the Omani Air Force based at nearby Salalah, and it would also stop any SAS reinforcements being flown in by helicopter. Like all guerrilla groups, the *adoo* had a pretty good intelligence network operating, and they knew when SAS teams were being rotated. The Omanis are notorious gossipers, and although the SAS men used the grapevine for their own use, there was nothing they could do to stop the reverse happening.'

The SAS team at Mirbat was not entirely alone. Other forces defending Mirbat included 30 *askars* (tribesmen) holding the Wali's Fort and 25 gendarmes occupying the Dhofar Gendarmerie Fort. These units were armed for the most part with aged bolt-action Lee-Enfield rifles, but worse was the fact that some of the *adoo* had allowed themselves to be spotted by the defenders, who had despatched a 60-strong *firqat* to investigate, further weakening the garrison. Among the heavier weapons possessed by the defenders was an old 25-pounder field gun in a sandbagged pit beside the Gendarmerie Fort, and an 81mm mortar in a sandbagged pit beside the Batthouse, the BAT Team's HQ. On the roof of the Batthouse was a GPMG and a 0.5in Browning heavy machine gun:

'Just before dawn on 19 July, the team's relief day, the day when they would be out of Mirbat for good, the *adoo* began their attack. It was just before 0530 hours, the time when they could make the maximum use of the uncertain light which, combined with the poor weather, meant it was almost

Right: SAS men unload a Beverley transport aircraft in Oman under the watchful eye of a comrade.

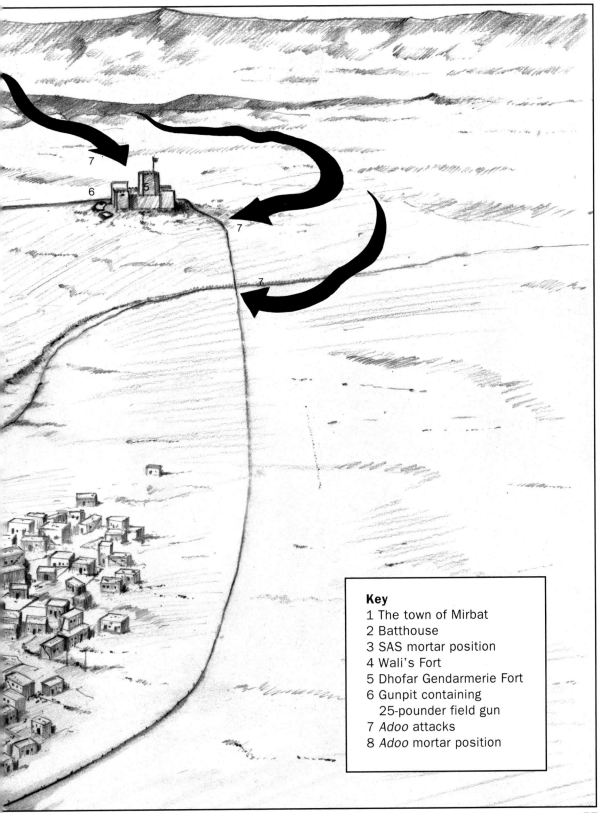

Key
1 The town of Mirbat
2 Batthouse
3 SAS mortar position
4 Wali's Fort
5 Dhofar Gendarmerie Fort
6 Gunpit containing
   25-pounder field gun
7 *Adoo* attacks
8 *Adoo* mortar position

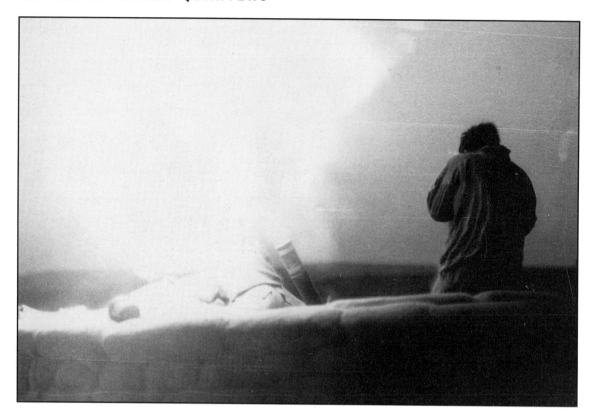

Above: An SAS 81mm mortar, similar to the one used at Mirbat, pounds *adoo* positions in Oman.

impossible for the sentries to spot their stealthy advance.

'Some 1000m north of the perimeter wire which protected the team's area (a sort of barbed wire cattle fence), the *adoo* cut down eight Dhofar gendarmes who were patrolling on the Jebel Ali. Poor bastards never had a chance, they only had old Lee-Enfields and they wouldn't have even seen the enemy coming for them. The distinctive noise of AK-47s echoed across the valley, alerting the SAS men to the enemy's presence. At first they didn't realise the extent of the attack, but Kealy rushed to the roof of the Batthouse to see what was happening.

'The SAS soldiers scanned the scene. The Wali's Fort was near the shoreline of Mirbat Bay and contained the *askars*. To the northeast lay the Gendarmerie Fort, which held around 25 men, though they were only armed with Lee-Enfields. Suddenly the *adoo* appeared, ghost-like, out of the early morning haze: lines of men

armed with automatic rifles advancing steadily towards Mirbat. Moments later there was a deafening roar of gun and mortar fire as the *adoo* opened up. The battle had begun.

'The odds were not very good. On the roof were Captain Kealy, Corporal Pete Wignall, Trooper Tobin, Trooper Savesaki and Corporal Roger Chapman. They had two machine guns on the roof: a GPMG and a Browning .5in, and they were to play a crucial part in the battle. Beside the Batthouse, in a sandbagged pit, Lance-Corporal Harris manned the 81mm mortar. As soon as the fighting had started, Corporal Labalaba, a huge Fijian, had sprinted over to the 25-pounder beside the Dhofar Gendarmerie (DG) Fort to help the Omani gunner load the beast, as well as give the terrified man some moral support.

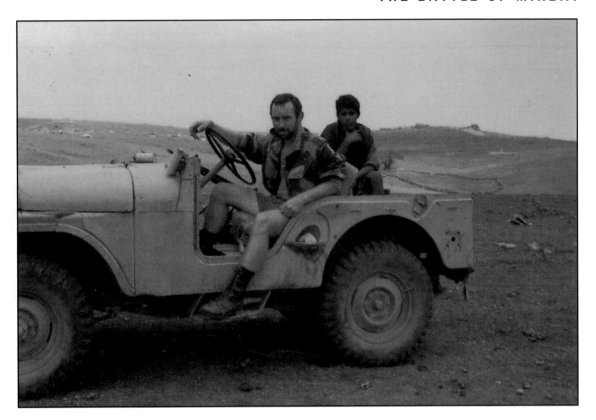

Above: An SAS Land Rover on the Jebel Dhofar. Because of mines, road travel was often difficult.

'Thump, thump. As the light began to improve the SAS men could make out well-spaced groups of guerrillas firing their rifles in a controlled manner. Hand-held RPG-7s were aimed and fired, their rockets slamming into the DG Fort. Then there was the sound of mortar bombs hitting the earth as the enemy gunners endeavoured to find their range. It soon became obvious that the *adoo* were directing their efforts against the DG Fort. They weren't stupid: if that fell they could systematically eliminate the BAT Team and their allies no matter where they tried to hide, as it overshadowed the town and everything else.

'By now the SAS had opened fire: the ripping sound of the GPMG, the deeper throb of the Browning, and the clatter of automatic rifles. The controlled fire from the Batthouse began to take affect: *adoo* fighters started to go down as they were hit by double taps and short machine-gun bursts, but still the enemy kept coming. All

the SAS positions were under heavy fire now, and the forts were taking hits from rockets and mortar bombs. The lone SAS mortar was replying, and in the distance the 25-pounder was frantically firing into the ranks of the enemy.

'On the roof of the Batthouse, enemy rounds were whizzing through the air and slamming into the sandbags as the *adoo* pressed home their attack. The SAS soldiers were drenched in sweat as the adrenalin raced through their bodies. Each man's mind focused on his training: stay alert, search for a target, think, think, only fire controlled bursts. The machine guns were exacting a fearful toll on the *adoo*, but still the enemy kept coming.'

The situation was not good. The *adoo* were hitting the SAS with all their firepower: automatic weapons, medium and heavy machine guns, mortars, 75mm recoilless rifles and a Carl Gustav rocket launcher. Kealy must have realised that this was no probing attack, the numbers of guerrillas involved convinced him of that. At the radio Kealy informed provincial headquarters at Salalah what was going on. The Wali's Fort, DG Fort, Batthouse and Mirbat itself were now all under fire from the enemy. Kealy was in effect surrounded on three sides. Undeterred, the SAS soldiers and local levies were fighting back, but for how long?

'Kealy requested an air strike, but he knew that it was a forlorn hope because of the weather – the *adoo* had played their trump card and it was working. Rockets slammed into the DG Fort, sending masonry into the air and leaving gaping holes in its wall. Then its tower disappeared in a pall of smoke and dust. By this time the walls were riddled with hundreds of bullets. How much more could it take?

'Over the radio came the message that Laba had been hit. The 25-pounder had gone quiet. Laba had been hit in the chin, but with remarkable composure all he would say was, "enemy are getting a bit close". Savesaki volunteered to get some medical aid to his compatriot. Kealy agreed. Savesaki raced off towards the gunpit. Bullets whistled around him as he dodged and weaved his way forward. The SAS men covered him as best they could, but he was really in the lap of the gods. And then he had made it and dived into the gunpit to relieve Laba.

'Kealy called Salalah again to request casualty evacuation. Then sudden quiet descended over the battlefield as both sides drew breath. The fight had been raging for about an hour, and each side needed time to reorganise and bring up fresh ammunition. On the Batthouse roof empty cartridge cases and spare magazines littered the floor. The soldiers were

drained and grimy. But there was no time for lounging about. Fresh ammunition was brought up and prepared for the second round. The sound of sporadic gunfire echoed around them as they waited for the next *adoo* attack.'

In the gunpit Savesaki had fixed a shell dressing to Labalaba's face to stop the flow of blood. The Omani gunner had been shot and seriously

Right: Sultan Qaboos inspects SAS and *firqat* fortified positions on the Jebel Dhofar. After Mirbat the *adoo* were forced onto the defensive in Dhofar.

wounded, and the 25-pounder's gun shield had been riddled with bullets. But then Savesaki was hit himself in the shoulder and head, and he fell back against the sandbags that protected the position. He was still able to fire his weapon, however, and as he did so the wounded Labalaba continued to load the gun on his own.

Kealy couldn't get in contact with the gunpit or the DG Fort, and so he decided to go to the fort himself, taking only one other man, Trooper Tobin, with him. The requested helicopter then appeared out of the cloud, but as it tried to swoop in to land it was fired upon by the enemy and forced to retire. This signalled the renewal of the battle as the *adoo*, convinced that victory was within their grasp, made their final push. Reaching the gunpit, Kealy and Tobin relieved the wounded Fijians. From the 25-pounder's ammunition bunker Kealy sent a radio message to the Batthouse requesting an immediate air strike. At that moment Labalaba was killed by a bullet and the rebels began to close in on the gunpit. Then Trooper Tobin was shot, and both the gunpit and DG Fort were being hammered by rockets and gunfire. Savesaki and Kealy calmly picked off enemy guerrillas, but then a grenade was lobbed into the pit and Kealy prepared to die. However, miraculously, it failed to go off. But Kealy still needed a miracle to save both him and his command. He got it:

'After Kealy and Tobin had reached the gunpit the *adoo* had attacked with even greater ferocity. Their dead littered the ground but still they kept coming. The SAS mortar was firing so quickly it appeared to be on automatic, and the barrels of the machine guns were getting hot. Then, from nowhere, two Omani Strikemaster jets appeared, streaking their way overhead and heading for the enemy.

being. The fact was that there were still loads of enemy guerrillas out there who would soon re-group and launch another attack. The SAS needed help, and quick.'

At Salalah there were 24 members of G Squadron, who were speedily loaded into helicopters and flown to Mirbat. A second attack by Strikemasters inflicted further casualties on the *adoo*, as the men from G Squadron, fresh and heavily armed with GPMGs, launched a ferocious attack on the enemy after they had been landed. The reinforcements were landed in two lifts, the first advancing inland and clearing enemy positions around the DG Fort, while the second group cleared areas near the shore.

By lunchtime the battle was over and the SAS had achieved a great victory. It had lost two men dead, Corporal Labalaba and Trooper Tobin, and two seriously wounded, but the cost to the enemy had been far greater: over 30 dead on the battlefield and many more dying of their wounds later.

Far more important than the physical losses, however, was the loss in prestige that the rebels had suffered as a result of Mirbat. They had lost many of their best men, and the fact that they had heavily outnumbered their opponents added insult to injury. Far from convincing the Dhofaris that the sultan and his British advisors were finished, the battle reinforced the credibility of Sultan Qaboos. The civil aid programme designed to improve the living standards of the Dhofaris was stepped up. There were more defections from the *adoo* and the SAS continued to take the war to the enemy. By 1974 the enemy was cleared from all the valleys in central Dhofar, and a year later the *adoo* were being pushed back to the Yemeni border. The Yemenis themselves, seeing that the PFLOAG was going to lose, began to withdraw their support. In September 1976, the SAS squadrons were withdrawn from Oman as the war had been won, but victory had been achieved not so much by force of arms; rather, the SAS's 'hearts and minds' policy had been the key to success.

They began to pour cannon fire into the *adoo*, cutting down some and sending others darting for cover. The enemy attack had been halted. Kealy radioed for Harris to hit targets near him, but they were so close that he had to haul the barrel up to his chest and grip the weapon with his legs before he could fire it.

'Then the aircraft were gone, but they had saved the day, at least for the time

PRINCES GATE

When a group of terrorists seized hostages at the Iranian Embassy in London in 1980, the SAS carried out a stunning rescue that confirmed it as a crack hostage-rescue unit.

The year 1972 was a turning point for Britain's SAS, although at the time neither the Regiment nor its political masters realised it. In West Germany the Munich Olympics were taking place. Security at the games was low-key, and it was thus relatively easy for a number of terrorists from the Palestinian group 'Black September' to take hostage and then murder 11 Israeli athletes. The outrage was all the more tragic because it was played out before the full glare of the world's media. For the West Germans the whole episode was a nightmare: once again Jews were being murdered on German soil. As a result of this disaster, the Federal Republic established what was to become one of the most expert counter-terrorist units in the world: GSG 9.

Many other Western governments, including the UK's, realised they were also very vulnerable to these types of terrorist outrages. Their capacity to respond effectively when a terrorist incident occurred on their soil was limited. Thus they too took the decision to establish dedicated counter-terrorist units. In 1973, a Counter Revolutionary Warfare Wing was established at Stirling Lines, the UK headquarters

The lull before the storm: 'Red Team' members photographed minutes before their assault on the Iranian Embassy. Note the sledgehammer carried by the man on the left.

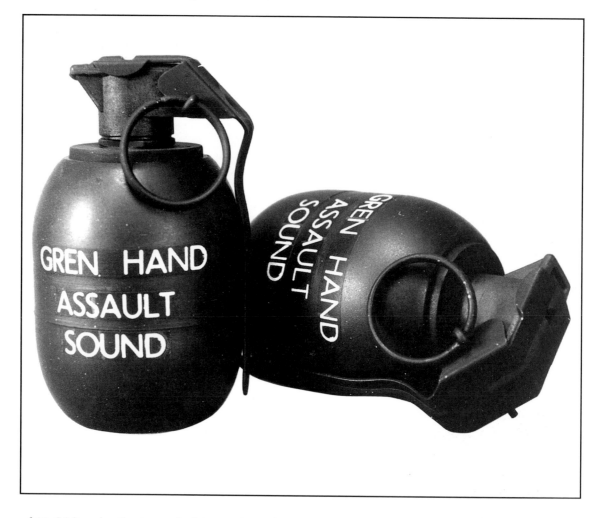

Above: Stun grenades, similar to the type used by the SAS at the Iranian Embassy.

of 22 SAS – the Regiment had been given the responsibility of being Britain's hostage-rescue unit. This was not really surprising. After all, the Regiment had always had a wartime Counter Revolutionary Warfare (CRW) brief. As applied to the SAS, CRW operations involve infiltrating areas by sea, land or air; gathering intelligence about the location and movement of enemy guerrilla forces; ambushing and harassing insurgents; undertaking assassination and demolition operations; border surveillance; implementing a 'hearts and minds' policy; and training and liaising with friendly guerrilla forces. Now, hostage-rescue was added to the list.

At Hereford every member of the Regiment's Sabre Squadrons was, and is, put through a close quarter battle (CQB) course, and a special building, known as the 'Killing House', was constructed to refine hostage-rescue skills. A member of the Regiment describes the sort of drills currently carried out in the 'House':

'Inside the "Killing House" live ball ammunition is used all the time, though the walls have a special rubber coating which absorbs the impact of rounds as they hit. Before going into any hostage scene or other scenario, the team always goes through the potential risks they may face. The priority is always to eliminate the immediate threat. If you burst into a room and there are three terrorists – one with a knife, one holding a grenade and one pointing a machine gun – you always shoot the one with the gun, as he or she is the immediate threat.

'The aim is to double tap [two shots fired in quick succession] the target until he drops. Only head shots count – in a room that can sometimes be filled with smoke there is no room for mistakes. Hits to the arms, legs and body will be discounted, and constant drills are required to ensure shooting standards are high. If the front man of the team has a problem with his primary weapon, which is usually a Heckler & Koch MP5 submachine gun, he will hold it to his left, drop down on one

knee and draw his handgun. The man behind him will then stand over him until the problem with the defective weapon has been rectified. Then the point man will tap his mate's weapon or shout "close", indicating that he is ready to continue with the assault. Two magazines are usually carried on the weapon, but magnetic clips are used as opposed to tape. Though most of the time only one mag is required, having two together is useful because the additional weight can stop the weapon pulling into the air when firing.

'The aim is to slowly polish your skills as a team so that everyone is trained up to the same level, thinking on the same wave length and aware of each other's actions. The "House" is full of corridors, small

Below: The Heckler & Koch MP5K submachine gun, as used by SAS hostage-rescue teams.

rooms and obstacles, and often the scenario demands that the rescue be carried out in darkness (a basic SOP on a live mission is for the power to be cut before the team goes into a building). The rooms are pretty barren, but they can be laid out to resemble the size and layout of a potential target, and the hostages will often be mixed in among the gunmen. Confidence in using live ammunition is developed by using "live" hostages, who are drawn from the teams (the men wear body armour but no helmets). They usually sit at a table or stand on a marked spot, waiting to be "rescued". The CQB range also includes electronically operated figures that can be controlled by the training staff. At a basic level, for example, three figures will have their backs to you as you enter the room. Suddenly, all three will turn and one will be armed. In that split second you must make the right assessment and target the correct "body" – if you don't you will "kill" a hostage and the gunman will "kill" you.

'A variety of situations can be developed by the instructors. For example, they may tell the team leaders to stand down minutes before a rescue drill starts, forcing the team members to go through on their own. Other "funnies" include smoke, gas, obstacles to separate team members from their colleagues, as well as loudspeakers to simulate crowd noises and shouting.

'New weapons and ammunition are continually being tested in the "House", and among the latest introductions is a new fragmentation round. It explodes on impact, so if a team has to storm a boat it will hit the bulkheads and burst without ricocheting, unlike ball rounds.

'Speed, fast reactions and slick drills are the key during CQB drills. Four-man assault groups are normally split into two teams of two, and each man is given specific areas inside each room to clear.'

By the late 1970s the SAS was fully trained in hostage-rescue tactics. As usual, the Regiment

had approached its new role with determination and thoroughness. Two of its men, Major Alastair Morrison and Sergeant Barry Davies, had taken part in the dramatic rescue of German hostages by GSG 9 at Mogadishu, Somalia, in 1977, and numerous cross-training exercises had been undertaken with the American Delta Force and France's GIGN. The Regiment felt confident that it could tackle a hostage-rescue scenario, but of course there was a nagging doubt about how the training would stand up in a real incident. There was only one way to tell if the SAS was fully prepared: if a hostage situation occurred somewhere in the United Kingdom. In May 1980, one did.

On the morning of 30 April 1980, six armed terrorists of the Democratic Revolutionary Front for the Liberation of Arabistan (a region of Iran not peopled by Iranians but by ethnic Arabs) burst into the Iranian Embassy at No 16 Princes Gate, London, and seized 22 hostages. The terrorists were armed with Skorpion submachine guns, Browning automatic handguns and Soviet-made grenades. The Iraqi-backed terrorists then issued their demands: the release of 92 Arabs being held in Iranian jails and a safe passage for themselves once this had been achieved. If the authorities didn't obey these demands, hostages would start dying.

As police negotiators began the tortuous task of calming the situation and wearing down the terrorists over the telephone, specialist units began to arrive at the scene to seal off the immediate area: D11 police marksmen, C13 anti-terrorist officers, the Special Patrol Group, and members of C7, Scotland Yard's Technical Support Branch. However, these were only supporting actors in the drama: the central players had yet to arrive.

A Special Projects Team was immediately despatched from Hereford (all Sabre Squadrons are rotated through counter-terrorist training at Stirling Lines, and at any one time there is a squadron, divided into Special Projects Teams, on 24-hour stand-by for anti-terrorist and hostage-rescue operations). Codenamed 'Red

Practising hostage-rescue drills: clearing rooms with handguns and submachine guns.

Team', it consisted of a captain and 24 troopers from B Squadron. Also at the scene was the commander of the Regiment, Lieutenant-Colonel Mike Rose, who implemented an 'immediate action plan'. When it became clear that a rescue attempt would not have to be mounted immediately, a 'deliberate assault plan' was formulated, which would be put into effect at the time and choosing of the SAS. 'Red Team' was continually put on alert for an assault due to the terrorists' threats against the hostages. However, though nerve-racking, they turned out to be false alarms. Reinforcements in the shape of 'Blue Team' (another 25 men) arrived during the afternoon of 2 May. Meanwhile, the negotiations went on.

As they were doing so, both SAS assault teams studied every scrap of intelligence that could be gathered concerning the building. Microphones were installed by MI5 in the walls and down the chimneys (see diagram No 1), allowing the police and the SAS to determine the whereabouts of the terrorists and the hostages. A full-scale model of the embassy was constructed by Army engineers at Regent's Park Barracks. At government level, Prime Minister Margaret Thatcher consulted with senior members of the Ministry of Defence, MI5, MI6 and the SAS. These meetings, known as the Cabinet Office Briefing Room (COBRA), came to the conclusion that caution and patience was the best policy. Nevertheless, time was running out.

The government's refusal to make concessions, combined with the non-appearance of the Arab mediators demanded by the terrorists, made the atmosphere inside the embassy tense. The leader of the terrorists, Awn Ali Mohammed, codenamed Salim, sounded edgy and volatile as he spoke to police negotiators on 5 May. By early evening things were going seriously wrong, and several shots were heard from inside the embassy. Then the dead body of the embassy's chief press officer, Abbas Lavasani, was dumped on the pavement outside the building. Sir David McNee, the Police Commissioner, telephoned COBRA and

Shotguns, such as this Remington 870 pump-action model, are used to blow off door hinges.

reported that he was handing over control to the SAS. At 1907 hours, Lieutenant-Colonel Rose formerly took control and implemented the rescue plan. Operation 'Nimrod', the codename for the SAS rescue, was under way.

The story of the assault on the embassy and the subsequent rescue of the hostages is told by the men who took part:

'When we had arrived at the start of the siege, we had been told to be ready to storm the building within 15 minutes. This would mean going in using firearms, stun grenades and CS gas and trying to reach the hostages before they were killed. At that stage we had no idea of the hostages' whereabouts. I looked at the embassy and thought of clearing 50 rooms one by one, while all the time looking out for the terrorists and their prisoners. Fucking nightmare.

'However, because the negotiators did their stuff, we were given a few days in which to prepare a more comprehensive plan, and we spent the time familiarising ourselves with every part of the building. The plan, like most good ones, was fairly simple: "Red Team" would enter and tackle the top half of the building, while "Blue Team" would clear the lower half of the embassy. We would also have the support of a multitude of snipers, which gave me, for one, a reassuring feeling.'

On the roof 'Red Team' waited like a coiled spring. The plan was for two teams of four men to abseil down to the second floor balcony at the back of the building, another group to assault the third floor, while more men would blow in the skylight on the fourth floor to enter the building that way. 'Blue Team' was tasked with clearing the basement, ground and first floors. 'Red Team' began the operation, but then almost wrecked it:

'We were on the roof waiting for the order to go. We had all made our last-minute checks – respirators, weapons, assault suits and stun grenades – and now we wanted to be off. The adrenalin rush was unbelievable. The word was given and we started to descend from the roof. I fed the rope through my descender as we moved quickly and silently down the side of the rear of the building. Then, disaster. The boss got snagged in his harness. Some of the lads tried to help him, but then one of them accidentally broke a window with his foot. Shit!

'All hell broke loose as orders were screamed over the command net to storm the building. Snipers started firing CS gas into the embassy. We couldn't get the boss free. Looking down I saw the lads from "Blue Team" using sledgehammers to break the glass and get in. The sound of gunfire filled the air as black-suited individuals started disappearing into the embassy. Jesus, what chaos!'

At the front of the building, on the first-floor balcony, a four-man SAS team placed a special frame charge against the windows. But before it could be detonated the men had to yell at one of the hostages, BBC man Sim Harris, to back away from the window inside the embassy. After a few seconds there was a terrific explosion as the frame charge was detonated:

'Then we were in. We threw in stun grenades and then quickly followed. There was a thundering bang and a blinding flash as the stun grenades went off. Designed to disorientate any hostiles who were in the room, they were a godsend. No one in here, good. I looked round, the stun grenades had set light to the curtains, not so good. No time to stop and put out the fire. Keep moving. We swept the room, then heard shouts coming from another office. We hurried towards the noise, and burst in to see one of the terrorists struggling with the copper who had been on duty when the embassy had been seized: PC Lock. One of the lads rushed forward

A brief glimpse of one of the terrorists at the front door of the embassy as he picks up some food.

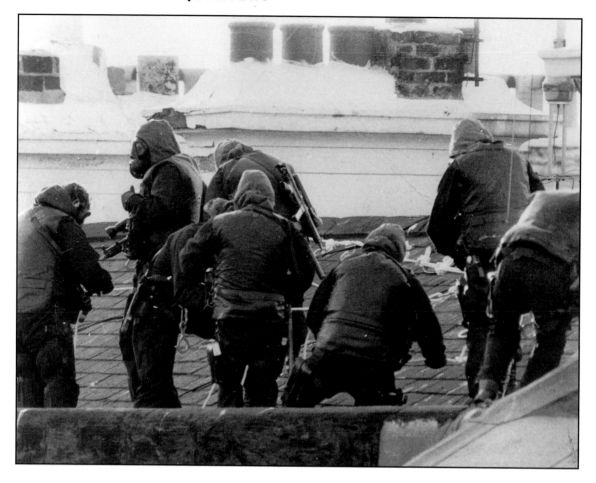

Above: SAS soldiers on the roof of the embassy conduct their final checks before the assault.

and got Lock away, then pumped a long burst from his MP5 into the terrorist. The bullets hit his head and chest, sending his lifeless body sprawling against the wall. One down, five to go.

'Lock was bundled out and we continued our search. The building was filling with CS gas and smoke. We had to free the hostages and get out as quickly as possible. Where the fuck were they?'

Originally it was thought the hostages were being held in an office at the rear of the building, and 'Red Team' expected to find them there as the troopers smashed the glass and then hurled in stun grenades. But the rooms were empty. The SAS team leader was still caught up in his rope, and flames started to lick round his legs as the inflammable material inside the rooms was set alight by the grenades. Fortunately, one of

the second wave of abseilers cut him loose and he crashed down onto the balcony. One of the SAS soldiers smashed a window and hurled a stun grenade into a room containing a terrorist (see diagram No 2). The latter ran from the room, but the SAS man raised his MP5 and pulled the trigger. It jammed. The soldier then drew his handgun and chased after him. The terrorist ran to the telex room, where three of his companions had started firing on the hostages. The SAS soldiers had to act quickly:

'We heard the screams of the hostages coming from the telex room. "Shit, they're killing them all," I heard my mate shout. We raced into the room [see diagram No 3]. Fucking pandemonium.

There was a figure on the left with a grenade in his hand. One of the lads shot him with his Browning, a well-aimed shot to the head which killed him instantly and blew his brains all over the place. We ordered everyone onto the floor. The terrorists had mixed themselves in with the hostages, and the latter were now going out of their heads. The women were screaming as we started to bundle them out of the room. One terrorist was identified, pulled out of the line and made to lie on the floor. Then he moved suspiciously and was shot – can't take any chances. His body was turned over; there was a Soviet hand grenade in his hand.

'Another terrorist was shot trying to make his way down the stairs with the hostages. Keep moving. We forced our way into other rooms and began clearing them. Shoot off the lock, kick in the door,

stun grenade, wait for the bang, then in and clear it. Empty. Keep going, and so it went on. By this time it was getting

Above: Chaos at the back of the building. A tangled SAS soldier is helped by his comrades as the embassy burns. But the attack goes on.

difficult to see, as the building was filling with smoke and the CS gas was working itself into every nook and cranny. I changed my magazine for a full one. Then we received the order across the command net – building clear, hostages safe. Time to leave. I was caked in sweat and my mouth was parched, but I felt elated because the operation had clearly been a success.'

The hostages and the one surviving terrorist were bound and secured on the embassy lawn until each one could be identified. Five of the terrorists had been killed inside the embassy: Salim on the first-floor balcony, two in the telex room, one in the hallway near the front door and one in an office at the back of the building. Only

one hostage had been killed by the terrorists in the assault, and another had been injured. For the Regiment it had been a vindication of all the years of training for hostage-rescue operations, but the aftermath was both good and bad for the SAS. One of those who took part, known as 'J', who now works with a personal protection firm in London, describes the result of the siege:

'Princes Gate was a turning point. It demonstrated to the powers that be what the Regiment could do and just what an asset the country had, but it also brought a problem we wished to avoid: the media spotlight. In addition, for the first few years after the siege Selection courses were packed with what seemed like every man in the British Army wanting to join the SAS. We just couldn't cope with the numbers who were applying, and so we had to introduce extra physicals on the

Above: It's all over. All those evacuated by the SAS were bound and checked on the embassy lawn. One of them turned out to be a terrorist.

first day just to get rid of the wasters. The same problem affected R Squadron, the reserve, and the sergeant in charge was overwhelmed with recruits.

'Another problem was that everyone wanted to be associated with the embassy siege. So now, many years later, there are loads of blokes going around saying they were at Princes Gate. The security industry attracts them like flies. At the last count I had interviewed some 700 blokes who took part at the Iranian Embassy!'

THE PEBBLE ISLAND RAID

The Argentinian aircraft stationed on Pebble Island during the Falklands War posed a potential threat to the British landings at San Carlos. The SAS was therefore sent in to deal with them – the scene was set for a classic raid.

During the Falklands War, the airstrip on Pebble Island was used by the Argentinians as a base for several of their ground-attack aircraft.

The island itself, a small stretch of land some 35km long, is a desolate, windswept place. At the time of the Falklands conflict it was home to only five families, who all happened to live near the airstrip. As the island is situated to the northwest of West Falkland, the Argentinian aircraft would pose a major threat to any British forces that were put ashore on East Falkland. They therefore had to be destroyed before the landings could take place. The Special Air Service was given this mission. The raid against the airstrip took place on the night of 14/15 May 1982, but beforehand intelligence had to be gathered. Timely and accurate intelligence is crucial to the success of any special forces mission, and the one against Pebble Island was no exception. The following account is from a member of D Squadron who took part in the action:

A wrecked Pucara ground-attack aircraft lies on Pebble Island airstrip after the SAS raid. The loss of the 11 aircraft was a grave material blow to the Argentinians.

'At our initial briefings we were told that Argie engineers had landed on Pebble Island and were preparing the airstrip as a maintenance base for their aircraft, which had been flown in from the mainland to support the garrison at Stanley. This was confirmed when an RAF Harrier pilot, returning to *Invincible* after a bombing raid, had observed a Pucara taking off from the airstrip. The Pucara is piss-poor in any air-to-air encounter so our Harrier pilots weren't too bothered about them, but in the ground-attack role it's another matter. Designed from the start as a counter-insurgency aircraft, the Pucara is armed with two 20mm cannon and four 7.62mm machine guns. In addition, it can carry an external payload of 1500kg, including bombs, napalm and rockets. Against lightly armed troops who have just conducted an amphibious landing a small number of Pucaras could inflict a great deal of damage, so they had to be taken out.

'On 10 May, eight of the blokes from the squadron's Boat Troop had gone ashore in kleppers [two-man canoes used by the Regiment and the Special Boat Squadron] to assess the level of enemy activity, while on board the carrier *Hermes* a plan to launch a strike against the airstrip was put into effect. Some of the lads, ever the pragmatists, suggested bombing it, but this was discounted for two reasons. First, the civilians lived too near the airstrip. Second, the Harriers wouldn't have enough time over the target area [the two carriers *Hermes* and *Invincible* were situated well out to sea before the landings to protect them from any airborne attack] to guarantee all the aircraft would be destroyed.'

With all the problems inherent in an air assault, the decision was therefore taken to use D Squadron in a classic hit-and-run raid. To the public imagination and the media, this is what the SAS is all about, but to the men who have to carry out the mission it is an operation that is fraught with dangers and pitfalls.

'People just don't realise what's involved with these types of missions, and that goes for some of the top brass too. I talked to the guys who did the recce after it was all over and they were well pissed off. They were dropped on a remote headland several kilometres from Pebble and had to paddle across the open sea before they could set up an OP [observation post] on the island. However, the high winds made the sea journey a nightmare; you just don't realise how windy it is in the Falklands, even the gorse bushes are bent double by the non-stop wind.

'Once they eventually got on to the island they had another problem: establishing a "hide". In the open terrain this was extremely difficult, as the ground provided very little cover either from the enemy or the elements. It looks a lot like Brecon, ie very few trees and loads of gorse bushes. Mind you, at least on Brecon you don't have that bastard wind, well, not all the time.'

The observation party had three main tasks: to confirm the presence and number of Argentinian aircraft on Pebble, to assess the strength of the enemy in and around the airstrip, and to work out routes into and out of the area for the raiding party. Once in place, the OP reported back to *Hermes*. The news was not good:

'Our shore-based team confirmed there were several Pucaras operating from the airstrip, but the number of Argentinian personnel on the ground was difficult for them to assess in the limited time available. In addition, the routes to and from the objective were reported to be like the rest of the Falklands: bare and easily monitored by the Argentinians. Fucking great!'

The temporary home for D Squadron during this time was the carrier *Hermes*. When the ship left Portsmouth on 5 April 1982, there was a small party of SAS soldiers on board, along with a company of Royal Marines and some Special

Boat Squadron (SBS) personnel. More SAS soldiers joined the vessel at Ascension Island. When in British service (she is now with the Indian Navy and called *Viraat*), *Hermes* was essentially an anti-submarine carrier, being kitted out with Sea King helicopters and a small number of V/STOL (Vertical/Short Take-Off and Landing) aircraft. In the Falklands conflict she could also have fulfilled another capacity: transporting the whole of 3 Commando to the war zone. In the event, it was decided that *Hermes* would carry the helicopters and Sea Harriers and not Royal Marines.

Life on board was cramped to say the least (the ship was the headquarters for Rear-Admiral John Woodward, the commander of the main group of surface warships during Operation 'Corporate'), but the SAS soldiers struck up a good rapport with the aircrews of 846 Naval Air Squadron, who had three Sea King helicopters with which to support special forces operations. These would be the aircraft that would transport the men to Pebble Island:

'The aircraft had no special equipment in those days, although the crews did have considerably more flying hours and experience than other pilots. A big bonus, which we were all pleased about, was the sudden issue of passive night vision goggles to Navy pilots. This piece of kit, in its most basic form, looks like a pair of hi-tech binoculars, but it enhances any night situation into a green image of daylight to assist the aircrew's view. Ironically, this treasured bit of equipment, which was already widely in use with the Americans, was issued to the Somerset-based Naval Air Squadron by the Royal Aircraft Establishment just days before they flew aboard *Hermes*, leaving very little time for training.'

With all the available intelligence gathered, the raid was scheduled for the night of 14/15 May. Originally, the SAS had been given the task of destroying the Argentinian aircraft, their ground crews and the island's garrison. However, because of strong headwinds *Hermes* took longer

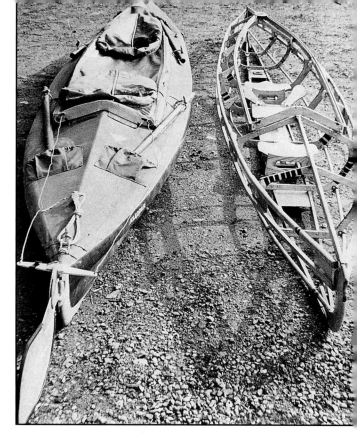

Above: Two-man klepper canoes, the type used by the reconnaissance team from D Squadron's Boat Troop during the Pebble Island operation.

to reach the flying-off point than expected. This meant that the SAS soldiers would have only a short time on the ground to carry out their tasks. The aircraft thus became the priority target. The Sea Kings would have to be back on *Hermes* before daylight, as she and her escorts (the frigate *Broadsword* and the destroyer *Glamorgan*) had to be well east of the island to minimise the threat posed by the Argentinian Air Force. The source continues:

'As we prepared our equipment and attended the first flight briefing with the boss of 846 Naval Air Squadron, this guy appears, he was a stores officer I think, and told us that we would never get off the deck until the weather improved. He had a point. The wind had been blowing throughout the day, which prevented the helicopter blades being spread on the flightdeck (below deck they were stowed with their blades folded). However, late in the evening there was a "weather window" which allowed the helicopter handlers, or "chocheads" as they were known, due to their habit of crawling under the helicopters and placing wheel chocks on the aircraft, to prepare the three Sea Kings for the mission.'

The Sea Kings of 846 Squadron are optimised as assault transports and are designated Sea King HC MK 4. Designed to fly in all weathers, they are fitted with a complete avionics suite which includes doppler navigation radar, auto-pilot and an auto-hover system. The fuselage can hold up to 19 fully equipped troops, and the aircraft can also be fitted with machine guns, rockets and rocket pods if required.

As the helicopters were prepared for the mission, the 45 men of D Squadron who would carry out the attack were given a final briefing:

'At the int briefing we were told that there had been more confirmed sightings of enemy aircraft operating from the airstrip. Additional information collated from some Royal Marines who had served in the Falklands several years before the invasion revealed that the airstrip was less than 100m from the nearest house, and that the whole area was flat and open, confirming our own information from the lads in Boat Troop. This made us a bit nervous, because if we were bumped we would have bugger all cover from enemy fire.

'The raid was given the codename Operation "Prelim". The plan was to use two groups to provide fire support for the raiding party, while another would seal off the approaches to the airfield. An additional fire group would escort the raiding party to the airfield and wait in reserve to react to any Argentinian anti-ambush party that had been prepared as a result of their watching us. The raiding party, or killer group, would hit the aircraft and plant explosive charges on them, or would use LAWs if an enemy presence prevented the charges being placed.'

The LAW is the M72 Light Anti-tank Weapon, an American throw-away rocket launcher. It is useful for SAS-type operations because it is light, which means several can be carried by one man. It is also accurate and can penetrate armour up to 335mm thick (though the version used in the Falklands by the SAS was only effective against light armour). Because it fires a high explosive warhead, the M72 is potent against targets such as stationary aircraft.

The SAS also had heavier support in the shape of an 81mm mortar and naval gunfire support from HMS *Glamorgan*, an air-defence ship for *Hermes*. The mortar had gone ashore with Boat Troop, though the actual bombs were carried by the men of the raiding party, who dropped them at the base plate before moving to their starting positions. Also put ashore was a forward observation unit from 148 Battery, whose job was to give exact coordinates to *Glamorgan* and then observe and correct the shelling as it came in. Following the final briefing, the men were issued with their personal equipment:

'Every one of us carried M16s with three spare mags each and an additional 200 rounds of 5.56mm. We don't usually tape a spare magazine to the one already in the weapon. For one thing, you can change a mag for one in a pouch just as fast as two that are taped together. And anyway, when you're in the field crawling through all the shit to get to the objective, such as mud and water, it all gets into the mag taped to your weapon. When you change mags and insert the spare one, all the shit gets pushed into the receiver. You then get a jam just when you don't want one, ie in the middle of a firefight.

'The M16 is a good weapon for short-range work because it's short, light and has a high lethality close in. It's not so good for long-range work, though, and it certainly doesn't have the stopping power of the good old SLR [Self-Loading Rifle].

Right: The briefings are over, all that remains is the long journey to the target in the Sea Kings.

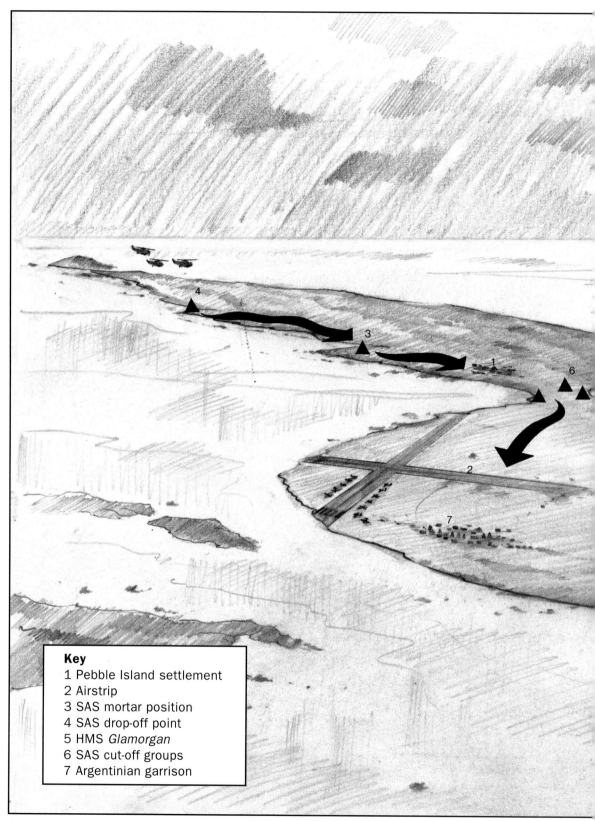

Key
1 Pebble Island settlement
2 Airstrip
3 SAS mortar position
4 SAS drop-off point
5 HMS *Glamorgan*
6 SAS cut-off groups
7 Argentinian garrison

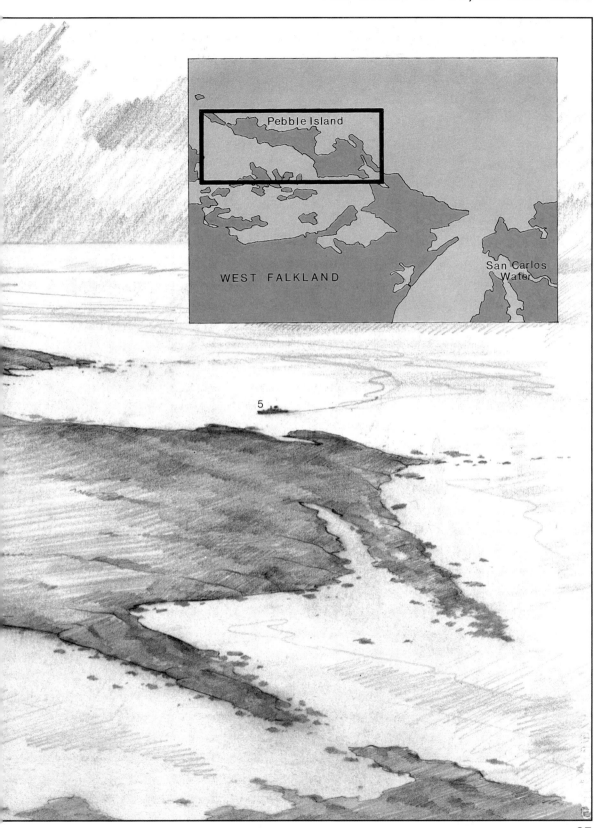

Pebble Island

WEST FALKLAND

San Carlos Water

5

Still, the weight saving over the SLR is worth it, and that goes for the ammo too, and anyway, for the raid we only needed a weapon for close work. We all took great care of our M16s as the weapon doesn't really like rough handling, which can be a bit of problem, especially in terrain like the Falklands where it's continually damp and windy. The Americans first touted the M16 as a self-cleaning weapon, and didn't even bother to issue cleaning kits. Naturally, there were a host of jammed guns when it entered service. They then issued cleaning kits very quickly, but not before several of their guys had been killed because of jams.

'Some of the weapons were fitted with M203 grenade launchers firing high explosive grenades. People get excited about grenade launchers but I don't see the point a lot of the time. OK, you've got a weapon that can throw a grenade over a distance of around 300m, which is a greater distance than a man can throw (even in the Regiment!), but the grenade only goes in a straight line. It can't go around cover, unlike a hand-thrown grenade. In addition, and this is something a lot of people don't realise, two-thirds of actual grenade tends to be the fuse, which means you don't get as big a bang as you expect. Add to this the M203's general inaccuracy, and you get the general idea. Still, for hitting a stationary aircraft at short range they are effective enough, and that's why we took them.'

Webbing and clothing are also important on special forces operations, and this was no different for the Pebble Island mission:

'The contents of our webbing is always a high priority. In addition to carrying rifle magazines and grenades, Falklands webbing included a survival pack, water bottles, a bivvy bag [a Goretex sleeping bag cover] and food. Each one of us customised our webbing according to taste. For example, a lot of the lads carried two '44 pattern water bottles with metal mugs, which are ideal for making a brew and

saving space. Waterproof matches are always a priority and are usually carried in small plastic containers, which are themselves waterproof. Each man will also have his own medical kit, though one person in the section will always carry a specialist medical bag. Syrettes of morphine are always carried around the neck for easy access, and two field dressings are usually taped to the webbing.

'Woolly hats are always worn, as a lot of body heat can be lost if the head isn't covered. In any environment, but especially the Falklands, you have to guard against hypothermia. We all wore climbing gloves, with the fingers cut out to make handling things easier, as a reserve. We all had white phosphorus grenades, with a good old nine milly pistol tucked under the arm in a holster. To stop us freezing our bollocks off we wore either green Goretex jackets or windproof arctic smocks, a lot of the blokes choosing the latter because they have huge pockets which can hold little extras, such as food.'

Though protection against the cold is very important, the Pebble Island raiders weren't over dressed. They still had to perform their task, and they were carrying a lot of equipment. If they were wearing too many clothes they would sweat heavily. This isn't a problem if you are moving, but if you stop then the sweat will cool, resulting in loss of body heat.

'We wore DPM [Disruptive Pattern Material] lightweight trousers. They are thin but they dry out very quickly after getting wet. Norwegian Army shirts have been a favourite with the Regiment for many years, and I wore one with a headover: a woollen tube that slips over your head and can be worn around the neck depending on the weather.

'Against the bitter wind a Norwegian Army shirt and a smock doesn't feel that warm, but as soon as you start to tab the body heats up and you're not so cold. Any spare clothing is stashed in the bergen. It's always better to wear fewer clothes when moving and to save warm, dry clothes for an emergency. Our bergens also contained binoculars, a tripod-mounted scope and night sights, the latter being a variant of the Individual Weapon Sight used in Northern Ireland. We each carried enough rations to last us three days, just in case we were trapped by the weather. Another very popular item of clothing was a set of quilted green trousers, which were ideal for zipping over your lightweights when lying up in a "hide" during the day.'

As *Hermes*, *Broadsword* and *Glamorgan* sailed towards the island, the men readied their equipment. Buffeted by heavy seas, the three ships made slow progress. *Broadsword*'s Sea Wolf short-range surface-to-air missile system became defective and she began to slip behind. *Glamorgan* sailed to within 10km of the shore to give gunfire support and to be on hand should the helicopters have to ditch. The carrier sailed to within 60km of the island, much closer than

Above: A Sea King helicopter, as used by the SAS.

was originally planned, to give the Sea Kings a shorter flight in the strong winds. As the hour approached for them to board the aircraft, the SAS men completed their last-minute checks:

'At around 2200 hours we made our way to the hangar. It was a hive of activity, as an army of engineers carried out maintenance on the tightly packed Harriers and Sea Kings to ensure there were enough aircraft for round-the-clock missions. We settled in a corner near the lift well, the huge mechanical ramp, with all our gear. A Navy mechanic asked me if I wanted a "wet", the maritime slang for a cup of tea, and I readily accepted his offer. Some of the lads drank, others smoked. It's funny, none of us discussed the job we were about to do, or the fact that some of us might not be coming back. We talked about home, football, the weather, our rations, anything but the mission.

'We made our way to the flightdeck. The Sea Kings were revved up, their blades spinning, as their aircrews went through their final checks. We sat crouched near the first aircraft, the South Atlantic wind combining with the draught from the rotors to lash us. My eyes narrowed to slits as I tried to stop thinking about the cold. If only the wind would fuck off! *Hermes* pitched and rolled in the heavy seas, her 28,000 tons battling with the ocean. Just as I thought I would be frozen to the deck, salvation. A "chochead" called forward the first stick. I heard someone shout "Thank Christ for that" as we rushed forward and entered the Sea King.

'Now the textbook says that the Sea King has a voluminous fuselage, and so it does if the team is wearing just T-shirts and shorts. But here we were, tooled up for the raid with bergens, webbing and weapons, which meant there was fuck all room for any of us. Thank Christ we didn't have any GPMGs or Milans. I wedged myself in a corner and waited for what seemed like an eternity before we lifted off. Then I began to sweat, shit!

'The noise inside the fuselage was deafening as the helicopter flew low over the pitching ocean towards land, skimming the waves to avoid detection by enemy radar. We didn't know if they had any on Pebble Island, but better to be safe than sorry. It wasn't long before we touched down on the island, and once we did we moved like fuck to reach the objective. We couldn't afford to waste any time, the old rust bucket *Hermes* wouldn't be hanging around, and anyway our colleagues already on the ground had established safe routes for us.'

The movement to the objective turned out to be uneventful. The Argentinian garrison on the island maintained a poor state of vigilance, which is surprising considering that they must have known that the aircraft would be a target. Nevertheless, the SAS soldiers were in a heightened state of alert as they advanced:

'I'll never forget the amount of sheep on Pebble. In Ulster, sheep and cattle are a major problem when moving about in the early hours. If you disturb them they will run wild, which will alert the locals to your activity. So here we were, moving towards the target with thousands of sheep all around us. Fortunately the guys from Boat Troop knew exactly where we could tab fast and where to move with caution. I had this vision of the Argies bumping us and a fucking great big fire-fight erupting with all these sheep being caught in the middle and blown to pieces.

'The mortar rounds we were carrying were dropped off at the base plate, and within an hour of being landed the cut-off group peeled away to take up position and secure the two routes heading towards the airstrip. By this time the cold was beginning to get to everyone. That's the one thing about the high command, they always find the most inhospitable places for us to fight a war in! I remember thinking how it was like being on top of Pen-y-Fan in winter, only in Brecon it is possible to move off the mountain and take shelter from the wind.'

There were six Pucaras on the airstrip, along with four Turbo-Mentor light aircraft and a Skyvan transport. There were a total of 12 Argentinian Pucaras in the Falklands, and if the SAS could destroy half of them it would be a big bonus for the Task Force. Both sides expected the Pucaras to take a heavy toll of the British after they had landed. However, the soldiers of the SAS had other ideas:

'The terrain was open and bare, just as we had been told. We approached the airstrip. I could see a large house to my left, which had a line of wind-battered trees to one side. I also made out some outbuildings and what appeared to be a windbreak for the house's garden. The area was riddled with fences and gates which were clearly part of a scheme to herd sheep into the pens around the house.

'I waited with the cut-off group before joining the killer group. Mountain Troop went forward, but then we spotted an enemy sentry and everyone froze. My heart started pounding and I tightened the grip on my M16. Instinctively, I slipped off the safety catch. We thought we had been spotted, but our luck was in, he didn't see us. We crept onto the airfield and laid charges on seven of the aircraft. Moments later the place erupted as we opened up with our small arms and LAWs. Using three-round bursts, I emptied a magazine into a Pucara, the bullets ripping into the nose and cockpit, sending shards of perspex into the air. Overhead para-flares from *Glamorgan* lit up the night sky. Where the fuck were the Argies?

'To my left a 66mm rocket slammed into the side of another Pucara, engulfing it in a fireball. The crackle of small-arms fire filled the air as the explosive charges started to detonate. I clipped a fresh mag into my M16 and looked around for fresh targets. By this time all the aircraft were either burning or had been riddled with bullets, their undercarriages shot away and their fuselages full of holes. In the background I heard the crump of artillery shells exploding as *Glamorgan* fired high explosive rounds into the enemy's ammunition dump and fuel stores. The opposition was nowhere to be seen. This is too good to be true, I thought.

'The forward observers had done a champion job. Now they were directing the gunfire to cover our retreat. We did a quick check on the aircraft, trying to identify them all and making sure they were disabled. When you're on a raid you don't fuck around. Time is precious. If you've achieved the element of surprise things go your way for a while. But in fact you're very vulnerable, and for all you know there might be an enemy battalion behind the nearest hill waiting to fall on you like a ton of shit.

'Then the raiding party and the cut-off team re-grouped and prepared to move

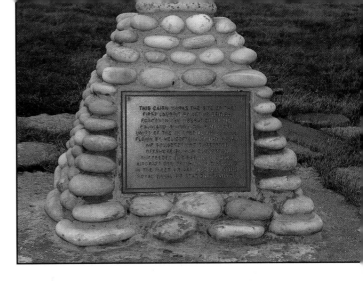

Above: The cairn commemorating the raid.

out. Just before we did, we received enemy small-arms fire. One of our boys went down. Instinctively we returned a hail of fire, each man firing controlled bursts from his weapon. Those that had M203s fired grenades at the Argies. It did the trick because we received no more hostile fire. We continued to fall back, more quickly now lest the enemy were re-grouping for another go. The wounded man was grabbed and hauled along (we never leave our wounded behind, it's an unwritten law in the Regiment).

'We bugged out at speed, reaching the landing site to await our lift back to *Hermes*. Bang on time the choppers came in, and a happy D Squadron was lifted out. I for one had expected a heavy firefight when we got to the airfield, but it never materialised. We could have hit the garrison if we had had more time, but as it was we all felt pleased with ourselves.'

The raid had been a total success. For the loss of only one man wounded, the SAS had destroyed six Pucaras, four Turbo-Mentors and a Skyvan. In addition, a large amount of Argentinian ammunition had been destroyed and the commander of the garrison had been killed. Far more important, though, was the fact that there were no Argentinian aircraft on Pebble Island to interfere with the landings at San Carlos Water, and the enemy's morale had been dented.

FALKLANDS: BEHIND THE LINES

Lying in 'hides' under the eyes of the enemy for weeks at a time, acting as a spearhead for conventional units, and shooting up enemy units – the men of the Regiment tell of their part in the Falklands War.

The British Falkland Islands are not a good place to fight. Logistically, for example, they are a nightmare, situated as they are some 13,000km from Great Britain. Thus when Argentinian forces invaded the islands in April 1982, the British Ministry of Defence was faced with organising a task force that would have to conduct an amphibious operation thousands of kilometres from home without the support of big carriers and a large surface fleet. In addition, there were no contingency plans. Military thinking at the time was dominated by potential confrontations that might take place on the central European plain between the forces of NATO and the Warsaw Pact.

A picture that amply conveys the type of terrain and weather conditions encountered by the SAS in the Falklands: cold and wet. Warm clothing, as worn by this team, is therefore essential.

There is also the climate of the islands to consider: they are for the most part cool, damp and windy, with a terrain that consists of treeless moorland and rocky hills; like Dartmoor, only worse. For special forces units such as the SAS, the geography of the area is a nightmare. Nevertheless, as soon as he heard about the Argentinian landings, Lieutenant-Colonel Mike Rose, the CO of 22 SAS, offered the Regiment's services to Brigadier Julian Thompson, the commander of 3 Commando Brigade, which would be the spearhead of any British offensive action to retake the islands. Rose had full confidence in his men's abilities, terrain notwithstanding, and in fact the Special Air Service was ideally suited to operate in the

Falklands because of its long experience against the IRA in Northern Ireland, as a member of the Regiment states:

'Our experience in the "bandit country" of South Armagh, Northern Ireland, served us well in the Falklands. However, there was one major difference: whereas the role

of intelligence gathering was similar to that carried out around Crossmaglen and Forkhill, the terrain offered little concealment from enemy observation. Our "hides" were in reality scrapes dug into the peat and covered over. They were, needles to say, fucking miserable.'

The first operation the Regiment was involved in did not occur on the Falkland Islands themselves. Operation 'Paraquet' was the codename for the retaking of the island of South Georgia, which is located some 1400km southeast of the Falklands. This is even more inhospitable, with arctic weather conditions and a completely mountainous terrain covered by glaciers. The British government had decided that taking the island would be an excellent way of demonstrating to the Argentinians that Britain would use force to regain all her occupied possessions. This was excellent on paper, but to the men who had to carry out the plan it nearly turned into a major disaster.

The small task force earmarked to take South Georgia comprised the destroyer *Antrim*, the frigate *Plymouth*, the ice patrol ship *Endurance* and the tanker *Tidespring*. Designated Task Force 319.9, the flotilla was led by *Antrim*'s commander, Captain B C Young. At Ascension Island the group was joined by the fleet auxiliary *Fort Austin*, which was carrying D Squadron, 22 SAS (the men themselves had been earlier flown to the island). Other forces included Special Boat Squadron (SBS) personnel and M Company, 42 Commando, Royal Marines.

An operations room was established in *Antrim* which quickly became the focus for a number of hot debates concerning the best way of retaking South Georgia. Major Cedric Delves, the commander of D Squadron, was particularly keen for his men to have the first crack. Some of his proposals underestimated the ferocity of the weather conditions on South Georgia, but eventually it was agreed that the squadron's Mountain Troop would be landed by

Left: A wrecked Wessex helicopter on Fortuna Glacier. The SAS's first operation in the South Atlantic, on South Georgia, was nearly a disaster.

helicopter on Fortuna Glacier and then move on foot to establish a number of OPs around the main Argentinian positions at Leith and Grytviken. On 21 April the men were landed on the glacier by Wessex helicopter.

However, it soon became apparent to the troop commander, Captain John Hamilton, that the mission would have to be abandoned. His men had made only slow progress before they had been forced to stop and camp for the night. They spent a thoroughly uncomfortable night on the glacier: the wind continually blew and the snow lashed their bodies and equipment (ice got into the feed trays of the GPMGs which made them inoperable). The next day three Wessex helicopters (one from *Antrim*, two from *Tidespring*) flew up the glacier to extract the men. However, one hit a 'whiteout' (where visibility is suddenly reduced to zero by the weather) and crashed. Fortunately the crew escaped serious injury, but this meant there were only two aircraft to extract the team. They landed and picked up the SAS soldiers and the aircrew, but as they took off one also encountered severe weather and crashed.

Despite this ill luck, all the men were eventually lifted off the glacier by the surviving helicopter, the one flown by Lieutenant-Commander Ian Stanley. His bravery and tenacity won him the Distinguished Service Order and averted a major disaster which would have been a grave blow to the morale of the Task Force and the British government.

Delves, however, was undeterred, and decided that the seaborne approach would stand a better chance of success. Therefore, on 23 April the squadron's Boat Troop, using Gemini inflatables, tried to establish positions on Grass Island. However, the bad luck continued: two of the craft broke down and were swept away by heavy winds (though the crews of both were later saved). All thoughts of taking the island were temporarily put aside as news reached the British flotilla that an enemy submarine was nearing their position. The ships scattered, bringing to an end the SAS's so far unsuccessful attempt to recapture South Georgia.

On 25 April, *Antrim*, *Plymouth* and the frigate *Brilliant* (which had reached the area the

day before) combined for a daring attack on Grytviken. Three troops were assembled for a heliborne assault on the settlement: one of Royal Marines, one of SBS men and another made up of SAS troopers. While *Antrim* and *Plymouth* pounded the shore (though they were under strict orders from London not to damage any of the buildings), the men were put ashore and moved forward towards the enemy. The latter was totally bemused by the sequence of events. The Argentinians were called upon to surrender, and while they deliberated *Antrim* was brought into the bay with orders to level the buildings if the enemy decided to fight it out. However, this was unnecessary: the Argentinians quickly raised a white flag and surrendered. The British soldiers who had been landed had won a victory without firing a shot. The men of D Squadron did not forget the contribution of the Royal Navy during Operation 'Paraquet':

'We were really pleased to have naval gunfire support when we were ashore, and when we returned to *Plymouth* to pick up some extra gear, we couldn't thank the crew enough for their help. They were the difference between strolling into Grytviken and having to fight our way in.'

The retaking of the Falklands themselves would not be so bloodless, but it gave the Regiment more opportunities to display its wide range of skills. Before any British landing could take place, the size, dispositions and morale of all the enemy garrisons had to be ascertained. This would mean inserting small teams of men onto the islands to watch the movements of the Argentinians. The first to go ashore were the men of G Squadron:

'We had been initially flown out to Ascension Island, and we soon got down to enjoying the sunshine and the beer. I think the high command must have been a bit worried that we were going soft because after no time at all we were heading south to the war zone. We travelled down to the Falklands in the fleet auxiliary *Resource*. As she wasn't a warship her crew enjoyed rather less cramped conditions than their Royal Naval counterparts, and we certainly appreciated our "spacious" surroundings.

'During the journey there was quite a debate about how we were going to be inserted onto the Falklands. Then this really harebrained scheme comes up whereby the whole squadron would make a HALO [high altitude, low opening] jump onto the southern tip of West Falkland from a Hercules transport. Stunned silence – we couldn't fucking believe it. OK we had steerable 'chutes, but in the South Atlantic wind there is no way you can make an accurate drop onto a relatively small bit of land after leaving an aircraft at an altitude of 10,000m. The whole squadron would have been scattered all over the South Atlantic!

Above: HMS *Hermes*. Her Sea King helicopters supported many SAS operations in the Falklands.

'Anyway, common sense prevailed and this idea was shelved. Instead, it was decided to insert both SAS and SBS teams by Sea King helicopters flown from the carrier *Hermes*. The Sea Kings were operated by air crews from 846 Squadron, who turned out to be fucking good blokes.'

As ever with SAS operations, the men were loaded down with equipment and weapons:

'Our bergens were packed to the brim with everything from waterproofs to quilted over-trousers, rations, communications equipment and ammunition. Everyone carried a LAW [the US-made 66mm Light Anti-tank Weapon], they were flavour of the month,

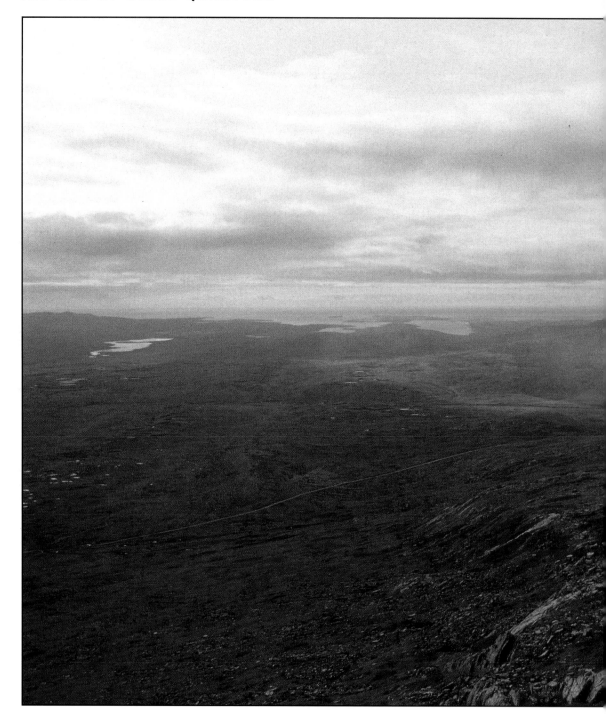

being light but packing a powerful punch, and once you'd used it you could throw it away. Other kit included mini-torches, a change of clothing, gloves, woolly hat, sleeping bag and a bivi-bag which

completely protected your "slug" (sleeping bag) from rain and sleet.

'As ever our belts never left our sides. They contained our emergency rations, water and personal medical pack, which contained everything from "anti-shit" tablets, which controlled severe diarrhoea, to strong pain killers that would numb anything from a mild tooth ache to a flesh wound.

Above: Typical terrain near the capital Stanley. One SAS team, led by Captain Aldwin Wight, established a 'hide' overlooking the town and was responsible for reporting a night dispersal site for enemy helicopters, which was then bombed.

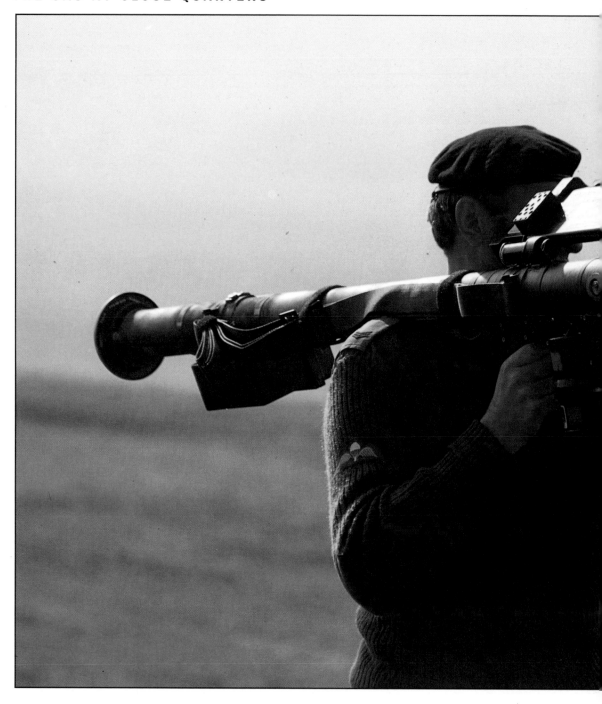

'We had a briefing that lasted three hours, during which time we were informed of the weather conditions, our drop-off point and the known dispersions of enemy forces. Afterwards we carried out our final checks and then ordered our evening meal. The crew of *Resource* did us proud and we ate like kings.'

One of Rear-Admiral John Woodward's primary tasks was to 'soften up' Argentinian positions on the islands through aerial attack,

Left: A Stinger missile. One like this was used by the SAS to bring down a Pucara near San Carlos.

'The insertion was to be carried out under the overall direction of the carrier *Hermes*. We were the first wave and would be landed on East Falkland under the cover of darkness (fortunately the pilots had night vision goggles to aid their approach). I remember the helicopter crewman looking at me with a look of total disbelief on his face as we loaded the bergens, he thought they were too heavy to lift, let alone carry across the island.

'Our hands and faces were heavily cammed up as we sped across the water in the Sea King towards our drop-off point. Inside the fuselage it was totally dark, apart from the reflection of the navigation lights on the pilots' control panel. The plan was for us to leave the aircraft as quickly as possible when it touched down, both to give us more chance of remaining undetected and to make the helicopter's journey back safer. The one thing you don't do when you're in "bandit country" is fuck around. To this end the bergens had been stashed in such a way that they could be pulled out by the last two who left the aircraft.

'Then we were over land and the signal was given to prepare for landing. The helicopter touched down and we were out into the cold night. We moved like lightning and the gear was off in no time. The crewman patted my arm and I saw him give me the thumbs up to wish me good luck, then he and the aircraft were gone. Then we were off, heading at speed away from the landing site (LS) in case the Argies had a fix on us and sprung an ambush. The rain started to lash down as we began our journey. We must have looked like a bunch of trolls, what with our heavy bergens, windproof smocks, webbing and waterproof gaiters to keep the wet off our ankles. After a while we made a quick stop to check our position before moving off again.

shore bombardment and reconnaissance of possible landing sites. He achieved the latter by using both the SAS and SBS, whose missions began in early May. The member of G Squadron continues with his description of the very first Special Air Service operation:

'During the march my mate whispered "what a god-forsaken hole this is". He was right. As the wind and rain buffeted us with an unending fury, my thoughts began to turn to Dartmoor and all the marches I had carried out across its miserable landscape. Yes, it was a lot like Dartmoor, except that the wind was stronger. My thoughts snapped back to the task in hand. We had four hours to reach the objective, which was 25km away. After two hours of marching we stopped and found a lying up position (LUP). We couldn't go any further because dawn was approaching and we risked being caught if we didn't go to ground. So we had to waste a day lying around doing nothing.

'The next night we set off again and quickly reached our target area and established a LUP and a forward OP, which was manned by two men during the day, while the other two would man the main "hide", ready to give covering fire if the OP was compromised. It was bloody freezing all the time, but especially at night, and the ground was so wet that it managed to soak everything through. As a result, it was impossible to be comfortable and so the whole time was spent operating in an unending gloom.'

There were many SAS observation missions conducted during the Falklands War, but a few will suffice to illustrate the kind of work carried out. One four-man patrol was led by G Squadron's Captain Aldwin Wight. His team was landed on East Falkland at the end of April and tasked with observing enemy movements in and around Stanley. He and his men established a covert 'hide' on Beaver Ridge overlooking Stanley and began their reports on Argentinian activity. They observed that the enemy had a night dispersal area for their helicopters which was located between Mount Kent and Mount Estancia. This intelligence was relayed back to the fleet, which despatched two Harrier aircraft to find and destroy it. The attack resulted in three enemy helicopters being destroyed. Wight and his men endured their conditions for 26 days before being relieved on 25 May.

Another OP was established in a wooden hulk in Darwin harbour, which was damp to say the least. Such daring could not always go unnoticed. One SAS 'hide' near Port Howard, West Falkland, was discovered by a party of Argentinians on 10 June. The men inside, Captain Hamilton, D Squadron, and his signaller, were quickly surrounded by enemy soldiers and called upon to surrender. Disdaining to do so, they decided to fight their way out. In the firefight that followed Hamilton was killed trying to cover the escape of his comrade, who was unfortunately captured shortly after. For his bravery Hamilton was awarded a posthumous Military Cross.

Life inside a 'hide' was invariably grim, and it is a testament to the mental fortitude of

Left: Captured Argentinians. The enemy proved incapable of stopping clandestine SAS operations.

individual SAS soldiers that they could endure such conditions for so long. In addition, the sheer monotony of each day was a great challenge to staying sharp. The soldier from G Squadron describes the daily routine involved in manning an OP:

'If we had a chance for re-supply one of the first things we would request would be thick plastic to line the shallow "hides" we dug. Anything to keep out the bloody wet. A four-man team would always establish a forward OP and an LUP some distance

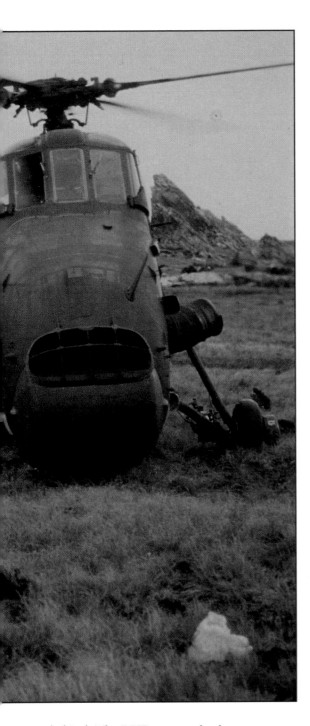

Left: A Wessex helicopter near San Carlos. After the British landings the SAS operated as a spearhead to support conventional units.

forward OP. The procedure in each team was the same: one man would get his head down while the other kept watch. There would be no movement or talking during the day. At night we would walk to the rear of the position and carefully cut a hole in the peat bog using a foldaway US-issue shovel – this was our latrine.

'It was impossible to cook during the day because the smell might alert a passing Argentinian, if one strayed that close, and so we only had a brew at first light. We would fish out a couple of tins of bacon burgers, or whatever came to hand, and put them in the water we were heating. When they were heated up we took them out and had the food, leaving plenty of water for a brew of tea or coffee.

'The weather was fucking awful, it was either raining, drizzling or blowing a gale, or a combination of all three. It was a real problem getting and staying warm. The wet was the real killer for me, I don't like being wet. We couldn't carry enough food to keep warm. During observation at night I would break open a bar of chocolate and eat it. It was like someone turning on the central heating, then, the next instant, you would be cold again. Bit like pissing yourself, really.

'Our first position was near Darwin, East Falkland, and the forward OP was situated near the edge of an inlet. Little happened at first, but after a few days had passed we logged enemy helicopters buzzing the ground immediately to our front. We stayed there 10 days before we received our first re-supply and fresh orders. The targets were really tasty, and it would have been very easy to take a pot at them, but our role was to sit and watch and that's what we did. Later it emerged that the aircraft we had reported were bringing in troops from Stanley to garrison the Goose Green settlement.'

behind. The LUP was nearly always situated on higher ground. This allowed it to give fire support to the forward OP if the latter was compromised and its occupants forced to bug out. There were always two men in the LUP and two in the

Something that comes across when talking to SAS men about their ops in the Falklands concerns the back-breaking loads they carried:

'In the Falklands it was a question of guys carrying vast amounts of everything. But they're was never enough room in your bergen or in your webbing and so there had to be a compromise. No one carried enough food, in the sense of keeping you well-fed, so a lot of the guys smoked because cigarettes dulled the appetite and were lighter to carry than rations.

'As far as weapons were concerned, it all depended on the task in hand. I remember one short-term job which involved observing the enemy where there was a patrol mix of M16, SLR, Colt Commando and GPMG. Each one of us also had a 9mm Browning High Power and as many Claymore mines and LAWs as could be carried. Each of us ended up humping around some 60kg of kit in total, which is bloody torture. I was carrying three types of ammunition: 9mm for the pistol, 5.56mm for my M16 (I had six fully loaded mags on me plus the one in the weapon) and around 1000 7.62mm rounds for the GPMG. In addition to clothing, rations and ammunition, every patrol also had to carry a radio and spare batteries.

'The ironic thing about the ammo is that we rarely used it, and we prayed that we wouldn't have to. The last thing we wanted was the Argies to spot us. All we wanted to do was go out, do our observing and then come back unscathed. In reality, if you had to fight your way out of a situation it meant you had let the opposition know you were there, which meant on an intelligence-gathering job you had badly fucked up. Having said that, in the back of your mind it was always satisfying to know that if you were compromised, you had enough firepower to give the enemy hell for up to three quarters of an hour.'

Despite the fact that there were some 11,000 enemy soldiers on the islands and 42 hostile aircraft and helicopters, both the SAS and SBS were able to insert teams onto the islands with impunity. Ironically, the most casualties inflicted on the Regiment during the conflict occurred during a cross-decking exercise from *Hermes* to the assault ship *Intrepid*. As the light started to fade on 19 May, one last journey was undertaken by the Sea King helicopter code-named 'Victor Tango'. Crammed into her fuselage were men from both G and D Squadrons. As the helicopter made one last circuit round *Intrepid* while its flight deck was cleared of another aircraft, something – probably a giant petrel – hit the engine and caused 'Victor Tango' to pitch into the sea. The crash resulted in 20 deaths, including 18 SAS soldiers: it was the Regiment's highest single loss since World War II.

Despite this tragedy, operations went on. In fact there were so many teams operating at this time that many of them ran into each other, with unfortunate consequences:

'Working alongside our cousins in the SBS, we were given specific areas to work in. The concept, as in other theatres of war where friendly forces work in a confined area, was to eliminate the danger of patrols running into each other. This scenario, known as "blue on blue", happened several times in the Falklands, and patrols would open up on each other until both sides realised their mistake. Fortunately there were no casualties, that is until an SAS team ran into SBS patrol. Exactly how they met each other is a mystery, but the consequence was a short, intense firefight in which one of the SBS men, Sergeant "Kiwi" Hunt, was mortally wounded. Great shame. He was one of the unsung heroes of the war, living ashore for weeks before the main landings.'

As the Task Force prepared for the main landings at San Carlos Water, the SAS and SBS were tasked with mounting diversionary attacks against the Argentinians. One of these was conducted by 40 men of D Squadron, led by Major Delves, in the Darwin/Goose Green area:

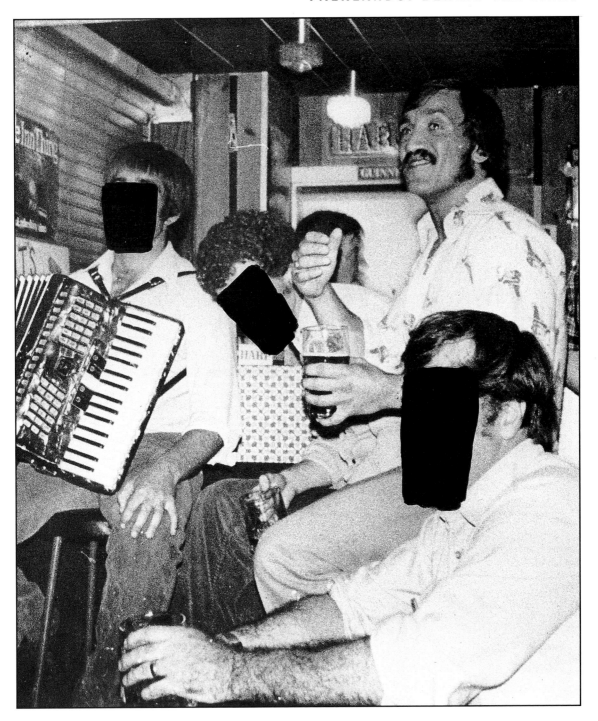

Sergeant 'Kiwi' Hunt (face uncovered), mistakenly killed by the SAS in a 'blue on blue' incident.

'We were still hurting from the loss of the Sea King, but we still had a job to do and just before the landings we were sent to keep the opposition's heads down at Goose Green. We knew the Argies had a sizeable garrison there but we didn't know exactly how many. What we did know was that we were heavily outnumbered. Still, we were armed with GPMGs, Milans, grenade launchers, mortars and a Stinger surface-to-air missile. Our orders were to convince the Argies they were being attacked by a whole battalion. We were told to "just blast them", though any close-quarter fighting was ruled out because if we got too close they would suss us. This battle would be from a safe distance.

'We were flown in by Sea Kings, each man carrying a fucking great big load of armaments. We left the choppers and had to trudge 30km to our positions: the low hills to the north of Darwin/Goose Green.

We stopped regularly to adjust our bergens, as well as the Milans we were

Below: Poorly led, their morale low, Argentinian conscripts posed few problems for the SAS.

carrying. The weight was unbelievable. I remember thinking it was a good job we were going to fire most of the ammo because I for one didn't fancy the idea of marching back with it.

'When we reached our position we spaced ourselves out and then the boss gave the signal to open up. The next minute the night sky was illuminated with tracer rounds as the GPMGs began firing. Then the 66mm LAWs streaked across the ground and found their targets, quickly followed by the Milans. The noise was deafening. We would move from spot to spot to give the impression there was a multitude of firing positions. The Argies never knew what hit them. They did return fire, but it was wild and inaccurate and we never took any casualties. God knows how many rounds we fired that night, but the enemy never ventured from their positions and we well pleased with ourselves. By dawn we had packed up and were heading towards San Carlos water.'

The British plan was to establish a strong beachhead at San Carlos and then strike across East Falkland to Stanley, the capital. The days and weeks after the landings witnessed the SAS and SBS supporting conventional units by conducting probing missions to locate enemy forward positions. At the end of May, for example, the Regiment seized Mount Kent and held it, before being reinforced by 42 Commando, and in early June five SAS teams were landed on West Falkland. But more than anything else, it had been the intelligence that individual SAS teams had relayed back to the fleet in the weeks before the landings that had been perhaps more valuable: SAS soldiers lying for days in cramped, cold 'hides' observing the enemy and knowing that if compromised they would face certain death or capture, but still carrying out their job with the professionalism that is the hallmark of the Regiment.

Left: The debris of war. All the battles are over and all that is left for the Argentinians is defeat. It is a British victory, in no small part due to the SAS.

NORTHERN IRELAND AND LOUGHALL

In this chapter, SAS soldiers describe surveillance missions in Ulster, how they spring ambushes on IRA teams, and what it's like to work in the 'bandit country' of South Armagh.

Northern Ireland. Two words that conjure up images of civil strife, bomb-scarred towns and cities, mutilated soldiers and civilians and a hate-filled populace. For the Special Air Service, Ulster has been the location of its most long-running campaign, one which appears to have no end in sight. It is impossible in just one chapter to provide a comprehensive history of all the Regiment's actions in the Province. However, by using the words of SAS soldiers themselves, an impression can be given of the type of war being fought by the Regiment in Ulster and the kind of skills needed to fight the 'unseen enemy'. But why was the SAS there in the first place?

A British Army patrol leaves Republican 'Free Derry'. The SAS also patrols the streets of Northern Ireland, its men usually in unmarked cars and wearing civilian clothes.

British troops were first despatched to Northern Ireland in August 1969 to stop the inter-communal violence between Catholics and Protestants. This period also saw the first deployment of the SAS, when members of D Squadron, 22 SAS, were engaged in the countryside to hunt for Protestant weapons. The war in Oman (1970-76) meant the Regiment did not have the manpower to maintain a sizeable presence in the Province, though individual officers and NCOs were posted there to carry out intelligence tasks. However, in 1976 the British government announced in the House of Commons that the Special Air Service was being deployed to the Province, specifically to South Armagh, signalling the beginning of a squadron-sized SAS presence in Ulster.

The main adversaries of the SAS in Northern Ireland were, and continue to be, the nationalist Irish Republican Army (IRA), which

IRA, was captured near Forkhill, South Armagh, though he was killed while trying to escape. However, this incident notwithstanding, the terrorist threat was not so easily dispensed with, and the SAS settled down to a long campaign against the men in black balaclavas.

What does the SAS do in Northern Ireland? In the main it carries out surveillance and intelligence-gathering missions and undertakes ambush operations throughout the Province. From the late 1970s, the SAS deployment in Ulster was as follows: one troop (usually 16 men) at Bessbrook under the command of 3 Brigade; one deployed to the Belfast area under 39 Brigade; one to 8 Brigade in Londonderry; and a fourth under the personal control of the Commander of Land Forces. However, in the 1980s there was a change in SAS deployments. The splitting up of the squadron had meant that the Regiment's effectiveness was diluted. The Army recognised this and pushed for the establishment of a single, smaller SAS unit, one that could be moved from one place to another at short notice if required. For its part, the SAS was also experiencing difficulties: each squadron tour lasted between four and six months, with a period of prior acclimatisation training and a period of leave afterwards. With only four operational squadrons, the Regiment found that its soldiers were rarely away from Ulster. For a unit that has to keep its men proficient in a wide variety of military skills, this was not desirable.

To rectify the situation, therefore, a new organisation called the Intelligence and Security Group (Northern Ireland) was set up – known as 'The Group' – which saw a reduction in the number of SAS soldiers serving in Northern Ireland from a full squadron to a troop of just over 20 men (Ulster Troop). By the mid-1980s, SAS soldiers were serving for a period of one year in Ulster Troop and were working closely within the Group with the 14th Intelligence Unit. The latter is a covert British Army intelligence-gathering organisation that was formed in the early 1970s and whose recruits are trained by the SAS. In the Group the SAS contingent and

seeks to drive the British out by force, and the smaller, Marxist Irish National Liberation Army (INLA). There is little SAS activity against Protestant terrorist organisations, mainly because these groups are not engaged in a war against the security forces. In the mid-1970s there was much IRA activity in South Armagh, but the SAS deployment there temporarily witnessed a reduction in terrorist outrages. In one incident, Peter Cleary, a senior 'player' in the

14th Intelligence Unit were commanded by a single officer. In addition, the actions of the Group and of the Royal Ulster Constabulary (RUC) special units were also integrated.

Before they go 'over the water', SAS soldiers undergo training to prepare them for the special conditions that exist in Ulster:

'The focus of training for teams heading for Ulster is rehearsing for covert ops. They will carry out procedures for getting in and out of "hides" and will practise photographing "incidents", and all the while they will be assessed and monitored by Hereford's training staff.

'I remember manning one "hide" in the Herefordshire countryside. There were two of us hidden deep inside a roadside hedge, with two more to our rear to cover us. Anyway, at 0700 hours two masked men came out of the house carrying several weapons. They then stopped in the

driveway, giving us plenty of time to photograph them before they jumped in a car and left. We were well chuffed, and when we got back to base the photographs turned out to be excellent. So there we were, feeling on top of the world, when the instructors pulled out another set of photos – of us. Unknown to ourselves, another team had been stalking us and, as the pictures showed, we had failed to fully camouflage our position. We were seen. If it had been the real thing we might have been killed. It put the shits up me, I can tell you.'

The key to winning the war in Ulster is intelligence. In theory all the military and intelligence agencies in the Province work with each other to combat terrorism. However, there are suspicions that many of the different agencies are at each other's throats. MI6, for example, often prevents the RUC's Special Branch from seeing certain information, and the RUC in turn often jealously guards its intelligence. The SAS was initially given the cold shoulder by both the Army and the RUC, as the two believed that the Regiment's deployment to the Province was an indication that their efforts were judged to have failed. Despite the veneer of unity presented by all the security agencies, this rivalry, bickering and pettiness continues.

In Northern Ireland the SAS operates as covertly as possible. In 1976, for example, in the SAS's first official tour, men from D Squadron were attached to 40 Commando, Royal Marines, for their tour in South Armagh. On the ferry to Belfast they were wearing green berets and standard disruptive pattern material (DPM) smocks, and several carried L42 sniper rifles. During this tour the SAS carried out no less than 31 operations against the enemy.

But who exactly are the opposition? The original IRA was an Irish nationalist group that was formed in 1919 and which was dedicated to an armed struggle in pursuit of its aims. The

Left: A patrol waits to be extracted by helicopter after an operation in South Armagh. SAS teams make great use of helicopters in Ulster.

organisation split into two groups in December 1969: the 'Officials', the old leadership in Dublin, believed that an alliance between the Protestant and Catholic working classes would bring about a united Ireland, while the 'Provisionals', led by hardliners from Belfast, believed the only way to achieve a united Ireland was to drive out the British by force. The Provisionals soon gained the upper hand, and to this day the IRA is also known as the 'Provos'. Its list of assassinations, murders and bombings is long, but notable atrocities include the deaths of 21 people in the Birmingham pub bombings in November 1974, the bombing of the Grand Hotel in Brighton in October 1984, and killing 11 civilians at a Remembrance Day ceremony in Enniskillen in November 1987. Most of the IRA's major 'players' are known to the security forces, but catching them in the act of committing a terrorist offence, the only way they can be legally apprehended, is very difficult. Nevertheless, the skills possessed by the soldiers of the Special Air Service have proved invaluable in the Province in arresting IRA operatives and preventing terrorist outrages.

The following account concerns an SAS operation in South Armagh in the late 1970s, and is typical of the type of work the Regiment is engaged in as part of the fight against terrorism in Ulster. It is told by a member of 22 SAS:

'Orders were given in the full Ground, Situation, Mission style of all operations, with background details on the target. He was a known 'player' who had been involved in an attack on 3 Para and possibly the Kingsmills massacre [on 5 January 1976, 12 IRA terrorists had stopped a workers' minibus at Kingsmills, County Armagh, lined up the 11 Protestant passengers by the side of the road and riddled them with gunfire – only one escaped with his life]. The aim was to take him out of the circuit and crush the morale of the young "bulls" in Cross [Crossmaglen], who were waiting in the wings to follow their leaders.

'Two teams of four were tasked for the operation and rehearsals were carried out at a base in Ballykinler. The maximum range we expected to engage any terrorists was 500 metres, and so live rehearsals were essential. The brief was headed by two senior "Ruperts" [SAS slang for officers], but the most important figure was the IO [intelligence officer]. He had been in the Province for four years and was on the ball. A model of the local area was used to highlight the terrain and locate potential DLBs [dead letter boxes, points used to drop off supplies], PUPs [pick-up points, pre-arranged rendezvous in case the mission was compromised] and DOPs [drop-off points], as well as routes in and out, including an escape route and the location of the QRF [Quick Reaction Force, an Army back-up].'

The target in question was a local terrorist leader who was a major 'player'. The plan was to catch him committing a criminal act and arrest him. The SAS source continues:

'Both teams were inserted separately. It is an SOP [standard operating procedure], whether by helicopter or Q van [unmarked vehicle], that when there are two teams they will always travel apart.

'I was with the helicopter team that lifted out of Bessbrook in the early hours and landed approximately 2km from the area. Our role was to go to ground and act as the support group for the primary team, and log anything and everything that moved and which might present a threat to the primary team.'

SAS four-man patrols, because of the intensive training received by each team member in weapons handling, can lay down a devastating barrage of firepower. The teams that were on this particular mission were heavily armed. They were in 'bandit country' and were taking no risks:

'The primary team arrived on the ground by Q van and had inserted themselves into the roof of a disused barn by first light. They were heavily armed with M16s,

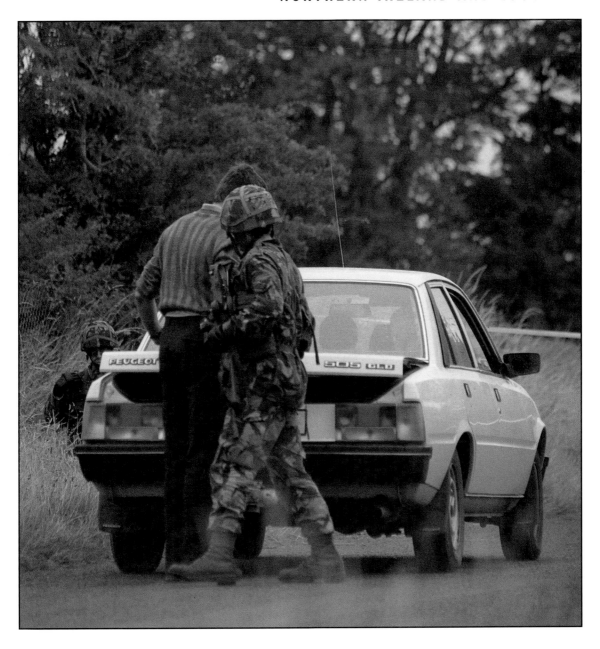

Above: An Army patrol at a vehicle checkpoint (VCP). VCPs are often used as cover to enable SAS patrols to secretly establish an OP.

shotguns and two M79s [grenade launchers]. In addition, each man carried a 9mm Browning High Power handgun. My team was equipped with a light machine gun, an SLR [Self-Loading Rifle] which could fire automatic and two M16s. The SLR man carried light machine gun magazines on his weapon, with his first magazine containing tracer rounds. If any fireworks broke out his job was to put

down instantaneous and continuous fire so the rest of us could see the tracer and use it as a marker.

'Each team was also equipped with a Sarbe [surface-to-air rescue beacon], which had one use: emergency only. For

example, if Paddy bumped us or we were
heavily compromised and couldn't use the
radio, then the SOP was to hit the Sarbe.
Another bit of kit, the strobe, was amazing
for bringing in helicopters: pilots could
locate it in all weathers and use it to find
the LS [landing site].'

Because SAS soldiers have to operate in all types
of weather conditions, they must have the right
clothing. However, the considerations of the
mission in hand must come first:

'Goretex wasn't around then, but waterproofs were out. We didn't wear anything
that made a noise. Boots have been a
problem since the British Army was
formed, and so many blokes in the
Regiment buy their own, particularly US
Marine jungle boots, which provide plenty
of movement for the ankle but still have a
strong base. But we all wore "goon boots",
which were small, pullover shoe covers
that had lumps of rubber on the sole. The
aim was not to leave footprints as the local
farmers, Fenian to a man, were quick to
spot boot marks and would pass the
information on to their mates in the IRA.
    'Everything was camouflaged: bergens,
weapons, the lot. We added a few extras to
our smocks, such as a large inside pocket to
carry a small radio and a few batteries. In
the main, though, we wore the same
uniform as other British Army units. This
was because if a team decided to break
cover, they would look like ordinary
squaddies.'

Though the SAS engaged and killed a terrorist
after three days of waiting, it turned out to be
another gunman, not the major 'player'. The
men were then forced to retire, having assumed
they had been compromised. This is a typical
example of the type of operation conducted by
the SAS in Ulster which, despite the intensive
preparations, can often end in frustration.
    Observation Post (OP) work forms what is
probably the main task of the Special Air Service
in Northern Ireland. The reason is simple: SAS

soldiers, because of their training and mental
and physical stamina, are ideally suited to living
in cramped, uncomfortable OPs for days on
end. Many OP missions are conducted from
Bessbrook, the headquarters for SAS
operations in South Armagh. A large former
cotton mill, it is now a hive of activity for the
British Army. Battalions serving in the South
Armagh TAOR (Tactical Area of
Responsibility) base their HQ staff and support
forces at Bessbrook. The support services
include Q cars and Quick Reaction Forces,
which can fly from the Mill's heliport to any
location in the area to provide instant back-up.
    The heliport, known as Bessbrook
International, is roughly the size of two football
pitches. The whole base is heavily guarded,
having been the target of numerous IRA attacks
over the years. An SAS soldier describes a
typical OP mission mounted from the Mill:

'After an intelligence brief at the Mill we
flew by Wessex to Crossmaglen SF
(security forces) base, where we were due
to meet one of our teams that had just
spent several days on the ground. Once
inside the base, we were briefed by the
company commander of the Black Watch
and an RUC officer. The aim of this was
to update us on their activity in the area
and the day's events at local level. Our
people passed on details about known
"players" seen in the TAOR, and the
movements of "targets" the Provos had
been monitoring, which was very relevant
to the operation we were about to mount.'
    'The deployment of the OP had been
sanctioned after intelligence from Special
Branch indicated a big hit was being
planned against Cross. In the past Provo
machine-gun attacks had scored massive
publicity, but their favoured method was
to use mortars. They weren't very
accurate, but Paddy would lob a few shells
in which would scare the shit out of
everyone and remind the British Army
that it was in enemy territory.
    'We had been told by the intelligence
boys that the attack would be very big,

and the Provos had even been boasting in the local pubs that at least 10 British soldiers would die, so the heat was on to prevent it happening. There were only two places from where the Provos could launch such an attack, the most likely being a football field behind the base.'

Establishing a covert OP is no easy task. A position has to be found that will enable the SAS team to view the target on a 24-hour basis, but the men have to be inserted into the OP secretly. In an area like South Armagh, where most pairs of eyes are hostile, this can present problems. Therefore elaborate tactics have to be adopted:

'A disused house on the edge of Crossmaglen provided the perfect position for a long-term OP. It was detached and isolated on one side of the road, with an occupied dwelling just 100m away. The obvious dangers of inserting a team into such a position required a check by an EOD [explosive ordnance disposal] team. We left Cross late in the afternoon as part of a Black Watch patrol, also taking three Royal Engineers along with us.

Below: A Wessex helicopter brings a team into Bessbrook. Many SAS operations in South Armagh are launched from the heavily fortified base.

'Wearing standard combat gear and helmets, we were part of a 12-strong patrol which headed out of the main square towards our objective. The aim was to acquaint ourselves with the terrain around the building which we were to occupy later that evening. We patrolled up through Cross, and at a given point the soldiers from the battalion established a VCP [vehicle checkpoint] on the Cullaville Road, giving us the opportunity to check the ground and the sappers the chance to clear the building. The walk-past recce was very useful. We were equipped with bergens, Armalites and a full-automatic SLR. If we'd have carried this gear in West Belfast Paddy would probably have sussed we were SAS, but in South Armagh, or 'the cuds' as the area is known, soldiers carry bergens and Armalites all the time.'

Constant vigilance is a feature of all covert operations in Northern Ireland, as the enemy has eyes and ears everywhere. In addition, what is standard operating procedure in large urban areas such as Belfast is not always applicable to rural areas and small towns and villages. Q cars and covert vans are not easy to operate in Crossmaglen, for example, because the place is so small and the base is monitored all the time by Republican 'spotters'. Therefore, the SAS frequently employs helicopters and foot patrols as a way of getting teams into OPs without attracting attention to the initial phase of the operation. Once established in an OP, it is a question of simply waiting and watching. The SAS soldier continues his description of the mission:

'We carried everything we would need to sustain a 10-day observation: water, food, ammunition and surveillance equipment, as well as a variety of "live traps" which we planted around the building as "insurance" against any Provos who paid us an unannounced visit. We also had an escape route in case we were compromised.

'Living in a covert OP for 10 days in conditions where you could be compromised at any time by noise or smell is very stressful, especially if your "hide" is near an inhabited building. Noise is a killer, and so a variety of precautions are taken to avoid compromise, and these must be enforced at all times if success is going to be achieved.

'After entering the building the bergens are placed in ready-to-move positions and are never moved again. Soft shoes, trainers or desert boots are put on and combat boots are stowed away – they are too heavy and are difficult to sleep in. We had one collapsible camp bed, which we had "liberated" from an American para, and erected it straight away. Cameras and night scopes were set up and plastic bags for human waste were put to one side. A second bag for empty food cans was also put to side. It is imperative to trap all smells – like noise they can literally be a killer. They can attract dogs and cats which will compromise the operation.'

Inside the OP there is little to do except to try to keep alert, for any lapses in concentration can be fatal. Though the men's lives are on the line, the temptation to take risks to relieve the boredom is great. Only through strict self-discipline can the pitfalls be avoided. This is where the SAS's training comes into its own:

'Smoking is out, and I remember the problems of trying to operate and sort out equipment in the pitch darkness inside the attic of the property. Even using a torch for a few seconds is too risky. The procedure was for one man to get his head down, one to monitor the radio, while the third carried out surveillance, this is all standard SAS SOP.

'Food is a real problem. At no time did we eat it warm, and the only time we had hot drinks was at first light when we could use a "bluey" with no fear of anyone being

Right: A plain clothes SAS soldier photographed in South Armagh. The weapon is a silenced MP5.

around to hear its gas burning. We drank tea – coffee smells – and ate a variety of cold meats and tinned food.'

Never far from the soldiers' minds are thoughts of being discovered:

'Camouflage cream is a must at all times for two reasons. First, although we could not see any broken or damaged tiles, a white face shines and might therefore be seen by a passer-by. Second, if someone accidentally entered the property and compromised our operation we needed the element of shock to surprise them.'

'Wearing desert boots, combat trousers, black roll-neck jumpers and woolly hats kept us warm, and gave us the opportunity to move about quietly. We weren't too worried about getting

Left: SAS soldiers undergoing a live firing exercise in Ulster. In firefights with terrorists, quick reflexes are the difference between life and death.

it is vital, and operational details such as DLB arrangements are made by whisper, again its an SOP which is instinctive. At night a team of ours at Cross mounted DLBs in which they delivered fresh sandwiches and supplies, such as radio batteries and other items, and took away our waste. This procedure centred on pre-arranged RVs, which often gave us the chance to exchange operational details and receive additional orders. Goods were exchanged or left in a bergen, and we in turn would deliver bergens full of waste, as well as 'shot' film that had to be returned for developing as quickly as possible.'

SAS soldiers are trained to fight as well as gather intelligence, and uppermost in each man's mind was the state of his weapons:

'Magazines on our weapons were changed every day, because a sustained period in an OP can cause the mag spring to seize and result in a stoppage. If this happens and the OP is bumped, you're fucked.

'In Ulster most of the blokes like the M16 because it can deliver more rounds than the SLR or even the new SA-80. It's also fairly small, making it useful for OP work in a covert "hide". A weapon that is gaining in popularity with the Regiment in Ulster is the Heckler & Koch 53, which is basically a scaled-down version of the G3 rifle, though it also looks like the MP5.'

bumped by the opposition because we each had a 9mm Browning High Power in a shoulder holster and our main weapons were always close by.

'To give us an arc of observation for the scope and camera we removed a small part of a brick, which gave us plenty of vision to monitor the road, the houses and the potential mortar base plate on the playing fields. Nobody talks during the day unless

Relaying information back to HQ can be a real problem for SAS teams:

'Communications can be a fucking nightmare, depending on which radio band you are using. VHF, for example, often interfered with local television sets when they were switched on and basically told the locals that the military were in the area. Thus if you are operating from a

property you never transmit during daylight hours if you can help it.'

Despite the nerve-wracking nature of OP work, there are still the mundane, everyday matters to attend to. These demand proper attention or the OP can be compromised:

'Our rubbish and human waste was bagged up and sealed all the time. Our urine was bottled and food packed in plastic containers, but the rats still found us. Rats are a major problem in OP work around Cross, and their presence can cause you to make noise in an effort to stop them attacking waste and refuse. The attic where the three of us lived was crawling with the little fuckers. They were big and would stop at nothing to get at the food or rubbish we had.

'We asked Cross to supply rat poison in a future DLB, which eventually resulted in a bag of 17 rats being shipped back to base in a bergen. The boys back at Cross thought it was some sort of joke, but in fact it was a real problem because we couldn't just leave them in the OP. By the time the operation finished we had returned more than 90 dead rats.'

'After several days your beard starts to itch, your hands are black and you smell. During insertion we had sighted a room full of hay and, in an inspired moment, had spread some on the floor of the attic to dull any noise and absorb our body smells. We were quite chuffed with ourselves. When we got back to Crossmaglen, however, after stripping off for a shower we realised it wasn't such a good move: our legs were covered in ticks and it took ages to get them off.'

Procedures for re-supplying covert OPs are continually being tested and re-tested, as they are

Left: A soldier from D Squadron, 22 SAS, on active duty on the outskirts of Crossmaglen in the 1980s. His ordinary DPM dress, lack of headgear and standard M16 rifle give no clues as to his unit.

vital and must be carried out efficiently if the OP isn't to be compromised. In the 1970s the DLB system was in operation, but the risk of this being a target for an IRA ambush meant the system has now changed to the Live Letter Box (LLB) method:

'The LLB system is much better. A covert car will drive to a pre-arranged RV with its rear window down (there's always two blokes in the front of the car), with another car, a back-up, some distance behind. Anything that has to be got rid of – exposed film, waste, wet sleeping bags – will be thrown onto the back seat of the car, while the bloke in the front passenger seat will pass the stuff requested by the patrol out of his window to the patrol members. Then they will be off.'

OP work is unglamorous, dangerous and tedious, and is perhaps not everyone's idea of what the SAS does in Ulster. However, it is vital to the intelligence war that is being waged against the terrorists, and is perhaps the best weapon in the armoury of the security forces.

Ambush operations are another part of the SAS's war against terrorism. They can be spectacularly successful, but they can also be controversial and raise the spectre of the Regiment operating a shoot-to-kill policy in the Province. However, the SAS is aware that any ambush operation will be subjected to intense legal scrutiny, and therefore impresses upon its men the importance of adhering to the Army's rules of engagement. An example of the difficulties facing the Regiment when springing ambushes is provided by an incident which took place in County Tyrone in August 1988.

In June, British intelligence collected an invaluable clue concerning a forthcoming IRA operation to assassinate a former RUC officer who worked in Omagh. The SAS, working in conjunction with the Army, the intelligence agencies and the RUC, decided to set an ambush to prevent the murder attempt. The identities of the local IRA operatives were known to the security forces: Martin and Gerald Harte and Brian Mullen, who together formed the Mid-

Tyrone Brigade. The intended victim was informed of the IRA's plan, and he agreed to continue driving his truck to work along his regular route to establish a movement pattern which would be observed by the terrorists.

The SAS plan was for the truck to 'break down', and then a team from the Regiment would lie in wait around it until the IRA hit squad arrived. However, the Mid-Tyrone Brigade didn't just have this operation on its books. On 20 August 1988, it blew up a coach carrying 35 members of the 1st Battalion, The Light Infantry, as it travelled along the A5 from Aldergrove Airport to the barracks in Omagh. The IRA team used nearly 100 kilos of Semtex in the attack, which hurled the coach 30m through the air. It was a devastating attack: eight men were killed, and many more were horribly injured. For the IRA it was a spectacular victory.

The SAS did not let the incident alter its plans: the operation went ahead as planned. On 29 August, the terrorists returned to their arms cache, indicating the murder attempt would take place the next day. During the early hours of 30 August an SAS soldier took the place of the target and drove the truck to the pre-arranged ambush point. At the same time, a three-man SAS team left the barracks in Omagh and walked to a derelict farmhouse near the village of Drumnakilly. They were armed with Browning High Power handguns and had 9mm Heckler & Koch MP5 submachine guns as their main weapons. When they reached the site one took cover in a barn while the other two hid in hedgerows on either side of the road.

At around 1900 hours the truck stopped outside the farmhouse. The 'driver' got out of the cab and unloaded the spare tyre to give the impression he had broken down. He knew the IRA would soon get to know of his whereabouts – the enemy had a host of eyes and ears in the area. Sure enough, later that day the terrorists hijacked a white Ford Sierra and, told of the whereabouts of the truck, made their way there. They were wearing black balaclavas, blue boiler suits and were armed with Kalashnikov AK-47 assault rifles and Webley revolvers – a heavily armed team out to kill an unarmed civilian, but that's what the IRA is all about.

The security forces had been trailing the IRA team on the day of the ambush to give the waiting SAS soldiers information concerning their whereabouts. However, the surveillance was abandoned when it was feared one of the unmarked cars had been identified by a potential hostile. The SAS team was blind. The SAS man at the truck, therefore, didn't realise who was in the white Sierra as it raced towards him, although his instincts told him something was wrong. He was right. He sprinted to a nearby wall as the IRA men opened up with a hail of automatic fire. As bullets kicked up the earth around him he made a frantic dash for cover, and made it.

The car screeched to a halt and the terrorists prepared to jump out and finish him off. At that moment a ferocious barrage of 9mm bullets hit the car as the three hidden SAS soldiers opened fire. The Harte brothers and Mullen were killed instantly, the Mid-Tyrone Brigade had ceased to exist. The SAS soldiers radioed for a Lynx helicopter to take them back to Omagh as RUC and Army units sealed off the immediate area. The operation had been a stunning success.

What was to follow was a public relations debacle, as the British government remained silent on the operation as the media and Republican commentators screamed that it was a revenge killing for the bus bombing. The SAS in particular was disturbed that no one officially contradicted these claims. Only belatedly did the Defence Secretary, Tom King, deny that the SAS was operating a shoot-to-kill policy. The operation was a brilliant military action which then turned into a propaganda victory for the IRA and its supporters.

A few months before there had been an even greater victory for the SAS, one which had gone down in the annals of the Regiment as one of its greatest successes against the IRA: the ambush at Loughall. In late 1986 and early 1987, the IRA had increased its campaign of terror in Northern Ireland with a series of bombings, beatings and murders. The Republican movement had stepped up its military activity in an attempt to make Ulster ungovernable. For their part, the security forces were on a state of high

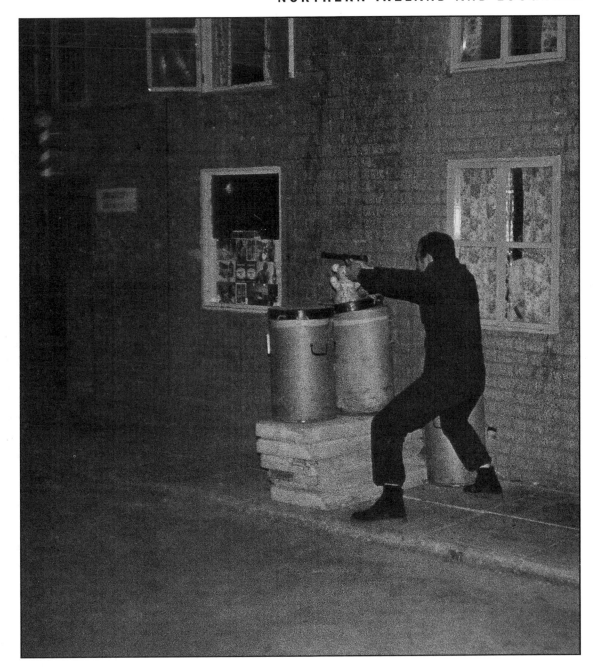

Above: An SAS soldier practises ambush skills inside a converted aircraft hangar in Ulster.

alert. But they received a godsend when, during routine surveillance, an IRA member was overheard on the telephone talking about a planned attack on the RUC station at Loughall, County Armagh, by the East Tyrone Brigade.

The East Tyrone Brigade was known as the 'A Team' within the IRA, and for good reason. It had carried out a number of daring attacks against the RUC and the British Army. In December 1985, for example, it had assaulted Ballygawley RUC barracks with AK-47 assault rifles and Armalites. Killing the two guards on the gate, the IRA team then raked the barracks

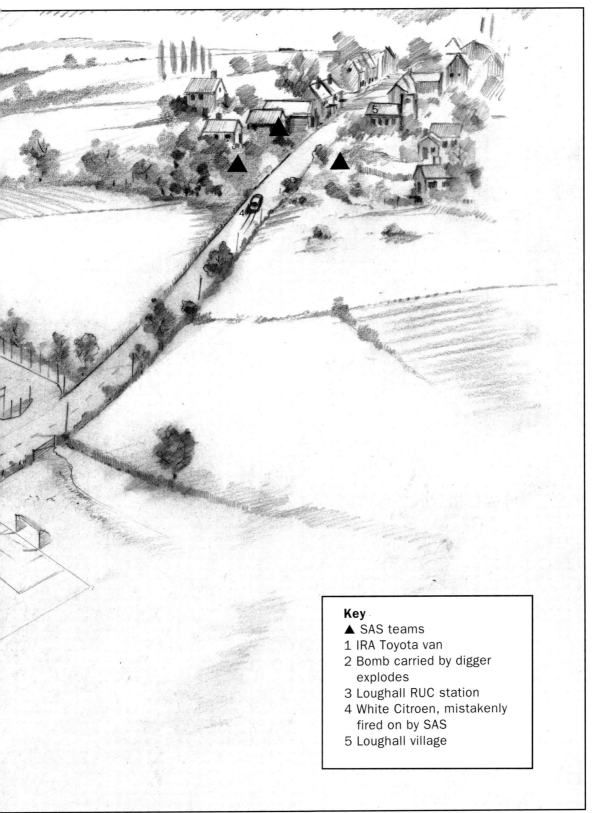

Key
▲ SAS teams
1 IRA Toyota van
2 Bomb carried by digger
 explodes
3 Loughall RUC station
4 White Citroen, mistakenly
 fired on by SAS
5 Loughall village

with gunfire before planting a large bomb inside the building. The subsequent explosion totally destroyed the barracks. The RUC station at the Birches, County Tyrone, was also attacked by the team. They loaded a large bomb in the shovel of a mechanical digger and rammed it against the wall of the building after first breaching the security fence. The explosion blew the barracks to smithereens, though the terrorists still felt the need to rake the area with gunfire after they had detonated the bomb. The attack on Loughall would be very similar, apart

Above: The aftermath of the Loughall ambush. Note the Toyota van and the remains of the digger.

from one small difference: the SAS and RUC would be ready and waiting.

Loughall is a small Protestant enclave in an overwhelmingly Catholic area. The village is a symbol of Protestant power, being the birthplace of the Orange Order. It had also been relatively untouched by the 'Troubles'; however, the IRA was determined to change that. The police station itself was a part-time, undermanned

RUC office, and the IRA planned to carry out an attack that would totally wreck the building.

The SAS was taking no chances. It was decided to reinforce Ulster Troop with more men from England. Therefore, the Regiment's headquarters at Hereford was ordered to send over more men. Soon afterwards, a 16-man troop from D Squadron was on its way to Ulster. Operation 'Judy', the codename for the ambush at Loughall, was under way. Because of the IRA's slackness, the authorities knew the date of the attack: 8 May. The SAS men and RUC snipers were infiltrated into the area many hours before the IRA terrorists were due to make an appearance. The SAS contingent was commanded by a staff sergeant from Ulster Troop, a man of great experience who would make sure the operation would be perfectly executed. At the prior briefing the men were told that the mission was an OP/React – an Observation Post able to React, a coded term for an ambush. The enemy would drive into a pre-arranged killing ground where they would be engaged and destroyed. The East Tyrone Brigade's luck was about to run out.

The SAS soldiers were heavily armed: those of Ulster Troop were carrying Heckler & Koch G3 assault rifles, those from England had M16 rifles, and there were at least two General Purpose Machine Guns (GPMGs). The men were deployed in two groups. The first, the larger one, was deployed in the copse overlooking the RUC station close to the Armagh road. In this way the soldiers, who also had the two GPMGs, could concentrate fire on the football field in front of the police station. The second group was in the station itself, with the men being at the rear and at the far end of the building in relation to where the gates were. There were also at least two cut-off groups in the village and another SAS unit close to the church.

There has been questions raised subsequently concerning the wisdom of placing men in the building, as it was known that the IRA bomb would be large and would thus damage the building and perhaps injure any occupants. Mark Urban, in his book *Big Boys' Rules*, believes the men were placed in the station because the SAS wanted to be seen acting within the guidelines of the British Army's Yellow Card rules concerning the use of force against terrorists, ie if the station was unoccupied when the IRA attacked it might be hard to justify killing the terrorists, because they did not present an immediate danger to life. However, with men in the building at the time of the attack, the IRA gunmen would be threatening the lives of security forces personnel and could therefore be fired upon legitimately.

Whatever the reasoning behind placing men in the police station, it did contain SAS soldiers as the IRA team approached its target in two vehicles:

'From my position in the copse I remember seeing the van slowly driving past the police station and then stop, followed some time later by the digger. There were three men on the digger and they all appeared to be armed [five more were in the van]. I eased the safety catch off my G3 and eased the weapon into a comfortable firing position. I could feel my heart pounding and the ardenalin flowing in my veins. Then the digger crashed into the gates of the police station and stopped, its bucket holding the bomb raised high. The terrorists then jumped from the digger and formed up in a line on the road. What the hell are they up to? They were all armed, a couple of them were carrying what looked to me to be G3s. Fucking good piece of kit the G3: compact, light and, most important, it rarely jams. That's the thing about the Provos, they always have the best that's available. Then they started shooting at the police station in an act of what could have only been bravado.

'Then our guys in the police station opened up with a hail of fire which cut down one of the terrorists. This was our cue, and the blokes all around me started to fire bursts. The amount of ammunition being expended was incredible. I began

Right: The Toyota van offered little protection to the IRA members who sheltered inside it, nor did the body armour they were wearing.

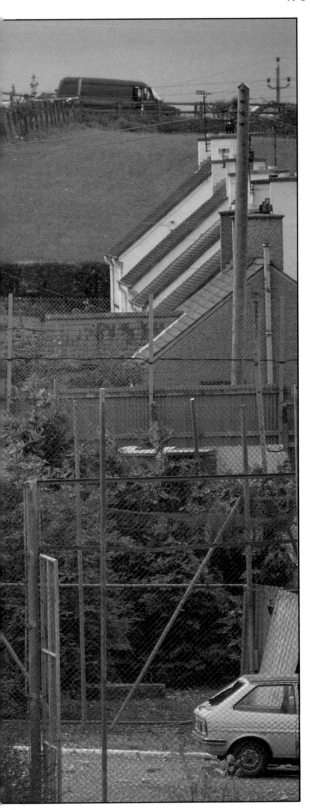

Left: The view from Loughall police station to the copse where the two SAS GPMGs were positioned.

firing my weapon. Then, Armageddon! The bomb exploded and the whole police station seemed to cave in. Everyone stopped firing momentarily, somewhat dazed, then, after what seemed like an eternity but was probably only a couple of seconds, we started up again as the dust settled. I emptied a magazine and clipped a fresh one in the receiver. The whole area was alive with the sound of gunfire. Two terrorists had tried to make a dash for the van, but were cut down before they reached it. Bullets were still hitting their lifeless bodies as they lay in the road. Another terrorist tried to escape from the Toyota by running across the football field by the side of the road, but he too was cut down.

'Bullets were spraying everywhere. By this time everyone was directing their fire at the van, and it was taking so many hits that I thought it would disintegrate (I saw it some time after the ambush, it was literally covered in blood and guts). Squeeze the trigger, squeeze the trigger, reload. I reached for a fresh mag and began firing again. Empty cartridge cases were flying all over the place, and in the background I could hear the rippling firing pattern of the GPMGs. I knew whoever was in the van would be dead for certain.'

All eight terrorists were dead. But the killing didn't stop there. Unfortunately a white Citroen car carrying two brothers, Oliver and Anthony Hughes, was fired upon by the cut-off groups in the mistaken belief that it contained IRA men. Tragically, Anthony was killed.

When the shooting died down the area was sealed off by armed police, and overhead helicopters scoured the countryside for any other terrorists who might be in the area. The SAS soldiers themselves, after ensuring there was no longer a threat, were evacuated by helicopter. The Regiment had just fought its most successful battle in Northern Ireland.

GIBRALTAR

In March 1988 the SAS shot and killed three IRA terrorists in a highly controversial incident in Gibraltar. The shootings prevented a major terrorist outrage, but why did the bombers have to die such violent deaths?

The incident in Gibraltar in March 1988 is one of the most controversial actions of the SAS in recent years. On 6 March three members of an Active Service Unit (ASU) of the Irish Republican Army (IRA) were shot and killed by four SAS soldiers on the streets of Gibraltar. The incident was the culmination of an intelligence operation conducted by British intelligence agencies, ably assisted by Spanish counter-terrorist organisations.

Following the successful Loughall ambush on 8 May 1987 (see Chapter 8), in which two ASUs – eight men – of the IRA's East Tyrone Brigade were killed by the SAS and Royal Ulster Constabulary (RUC), the British knew the IRA would mount a revenge operation. The question was, when and where? For the IRA it was, and is, much easier to hit targets in Ulster. However, greater publicity would be achieved if an outrage occurred in Britain or on the continent. There had been bombs going off and murders committed in Northern Ireland ever since the 'Troubles' began, and, to a large extent, public opinion in both Britain and Eire had become somewhat immune to the horrors there.

The Crown Colony of Gibraltar, a place that has been described as being more British than Britain, but where security is low-key. As such, it was considered an easy target by the IRA.

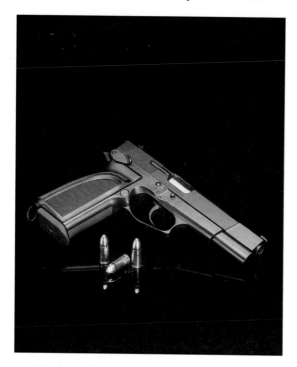

Left: The Browning High Power handgun, as used by the SAS soldiers on the streets of Gibraltar.

Gibraltar was a prize target, a location where the Union Jack flew proudly and where security wasn't as tight as in the UK or British bases on the continent. Following the SAS ambush of the IRA team at Loughall the year before, however, the British security and intelligence services were on high alert for any retaliation. MI5, the British counter-intelligence organisation, in particular, started to keep a close watch on the movements of known IRA operatives. Its diligence was soon to be rewarded.

For the Gibraltar mission the terrorist organisation assembled one of its most ruthless teams. First, there was Mairead Farrell, a middle-class, ex-convent schoolgirl who was one of the highest-ranking women in the IRA. She had served 10 years in prison in Northern Ireland for terrorist offences such as bombings and killings. Despite her angelic appearance, she was a cold-blooded operative who would go to any lengths to achieve her ends. Second, there was Danny McCann, the hard man from the Lower Falls area of Belfast. The mastermind behind a number of bombings and assassinations in Ulster, the RUC had linked him to no less than 26 murders in the Province. To the SAS he was known as 'Mad Danny'. In the IRA McCann

was known as an expert in close-quarter killing. He was, in many ways, out of control, a man totally addicted to violence whose only reason for existence was to continue the armed struggle against the British and their servants. Third, there was Sean Savage, a man who was the bomb-making expert. As such, he had the technical expertise the team needed. There seems to have been at least another team member, one whose identity has never been fully established, but who operated under the alias of Mary Parkin. Her task was to travel ahead of the team and gather intelligence concerning the target area, escape routes and when would be the best time to strike.

But to strike at what? Though there were several potential targets, such as the Governor's residence, various messes and the courts, the IRA's attention focused on a spectacular prize. Every Tuesday morning, regular as clockwork, the band of the 1st Battalion, the Royal Anglian Regiment, paraded up and down the main street at the changing of the guard ceremony. Around 70 bandsmen in full ceremonial dress performed the ceremony before marching off to a quiet square to disperse. In the square a bomb could be easily concealed in a car, for it was a peaceful spot and seemingly innocent. It was also well away from the main tourist streets, so large-scale civilian casualties would be avoided.

When considering the sequence of events that took place when the SAS soldiers engaged the IRA team in Gibraltar, it is important to bear in mind several factors before deliberating over the outcome. First, the IRA team contained dedicated, hardened operatives who were experts at their deadly trade. They were not amateurs, they would not hesitate to kill anyone who got in their way, and they would not meekly submit to being arrested. If they were carrying firearms, they would undoubtedly use them. This would be in the minds of the SAS soldiers as they moved in. Second, the actual drama was over in a matter of seconds. Events were dissected and analysed closely in the subsequent weeks and months, but it must always be borne in mind that the individuals involved had to make split-second decisions, and those decisions were taken at a time of extreme stress and fear. Third, the Special Air Service is not a civilian police force. It is a military unit whose men undertake a host of dangerous missions.

SAS soldiers leave little to chance: they cannot afford to. On operations one mistake can be fatal. In particular, all SAS men are highly trained in weapons handling. They spend hours on the range, honing and perfecting their firearms skills until they are second nature. Their reflexes become so quick that they can draw, aim and fire a full magazine of 13 rounds from a Browning High Power handgun in under three seconds. All memoirs of former SAS soldiers tell of the proficiency they attained with small arms. Michael Asher served with 23 SAS:

'We learned how to react to ambush in civilian cars, and how to take out terrorists in a crowded room, rolling and firing double-taps [two shots fired in quick succession] from our Browning pistols. We learned to shoot the terrorist and spare the hostage, to shoot in the dark and to clear stoppages.'

Adam Ballinger was succinctly informed of SAS philosophy during his Selection training for 21 SAS by one of his instructors:

' "This," said Scott [the instructor], picking up a semi-automatic, "is the fucking business. You may think you have passed your map-reading, but this is what it's all about." Scott stared passionately at the rifle: he had retrieved it from the strong-room and held it firmly. "Just as you would have failed the course," continued Scott, "if you'd failed the map-reading test, so we'll bin you if you fail your weapons test. From now until Camp, we will practise the drills over and over again. In this regiment they've got to be perfect." '

Dedicated, professional soldiers versus ruthless, veteran terrorists. When all the factors are weighed up, perhaps there could be only one

outcome. But in September 1987, when British intelligence services alerted the Spanish police of the possible presence of an IRA team in southern Spain, all that lay in the future.

In mid-November 1987, three IRA members were identified in southern Spain. They were Sean Savage, Daniel McCann and a woman named Mary Parkin. The presence of the three in the area meant one of two things: the IRA was going to attack a person or persons unknown among the large number of British citizens on the Costa del Sol, or there was going to be a terrorist attack against Gibraltar. One thing was certain: the IRA team was going to commit some sort of bomb outrage. This had been confirmed when Spanish police surveying the team heard them talk about a bombing.

The IRA team then flew back to Eire. The British still had no idea of the target, but that information was not long in coming. In February 1988 the terrorists resumed their activity: 'Mary Parkin' was spotted by MI5 in Gibraltar observing the changing of the guard ceremony. As soon as she had arrived in Spain she had been placed under surveillance by the Spanish. On 1 March she again observed the ceremony, and each time had followed the route taken by the bandsmen. In London, on 2 March, the Joint Intelligence Committee, which reports to the prime minister, was of the opinion that a bombing was imminent. It then notified the Joint Operations Centre (which includes an SAS liaison officer), a body that has the power to deploy the SAS. An SAS Special Projects Team of 16 men was speedily despatched to Gibraltar.

On 4 March McCann and Savage arrived at Malaga airport under false names. They were then joined by Mairead Farrell – the team was assembled. There were also other IRA members in the area. A white Ford Fiesta was hired, stashed with explosives and placed in a car park in Marbella (it was later discovered by the Spanish police). Another white car, a Renault 5, was hired on Saturday afternoon, 5 March, driven into Gibraltar and parked to act as a blocking car for the white Ford Fiesta that contained the explosives. McCann, Savage and Farrell then drove to the colony in a red Ford Fiesta, closely followed to the border by plain clothes members of Spain's counter-terrorist unit (up to and throughout the operation there was a high level of cooperation between the various Spanish and British police forces and intelligence agencies).

In Gibraltar itself the SAS waited. The men designated to arrest the terrorists on the street were Soldiers 'A', 'B', 'C' and 'D'. Their tactical commander was Soldier 'E', who was located in the Joint Operations Room, while Soldier 'F' was the overall commanding officer and senior military advisor to the police. In addition, there was Soldier 'G', a bomb disposal expert. On the street there were several MI5 watchers and two teams of armed plain clothes Gibraltar policemen, each one designated to support an SAS two-man team.

The two SAS teams comprised Soldiers 'A' and 'B' in one team and Soldiers 'C' and 'D' in the other. Each man was armed with a High Power handgun plus spare magazines, and was equipped with a radio-microphone in his collar which provided continuous communications with the Joint Operations Room. The actual plan had been carefully prepared and each of the SAS soldiers had been thoroughly briefed. At midnight on 5 March, there had been a briefing for everyone involved in Operation 'Flavius', the codename for the apprehension of the terrorists. Present were Joseph Canepa, Gibraltar's police commissioner, Charles Colombo, Gibraltar's deputy police commissioner, and Joe Ullger, head of Gibraltar's special branch.

The rules of engagement drawn up in London for use by the SAS were later made public by Soldier 'F' at the inquest which took place regarding the terrorists' deaths. They are worth examining in full, because they belie the notion that the SAS had a licence to kill:

OBJECTIVES

1. These instructions are for your guidance, once your participation in Operation 'Flavius' has been duly authorised. You are to issue orders in compliance with these instructions to the men under your command.
2. You are to operate as directed by the Gibraltar Police Commissioner or by the officer(s) designated by him to control this operation.

Should the latter request military intervention, your objective will be to assist the civil power to arrest members of the IRA, but subject to the overriding requirement to do all in your power to protect the lives and safety of members of the public and of the security forces.

COMMAND AND CONTROL

3. You will be responsible to the Governor and Commander-in-Chief, through his Chief of Staff, for the way in which you carry out the military tasks assigned to you. You will act at all times in accordance with the lawful instructions of the senior police officer(s) designated by the Gibraltar Police Commissioner to control this operation.

USE OF FORCE

4. You and your men will not use force unless requested to do so by the senior police officer(s) designated by the Gibraltar Police Commissioner, or unless it is necessary to do so in order to protect life. You and your men are not then to use more force than is necessary in order to protect life, and you are to comply with rule 5.

OPENING FIRE

5. You and your men may only open fire against a person if you or they have reasonable grounds for believing that he/she is currently committing, or is about to commit, an action which is likely to endanger your or their lives, or the life of any person, and if there is no other way to prevent this.

FIRING WITHOUT A WARNING

6. You and your men may fire without a warning if the giving of a warning or any delay in firing could lead to death or injury to you or them or any other person, or if the giving of a warning is clearly impracticable.

WARNING BEFORE FIRING

7. If the circumstances in paragraph 6 do not apply, a warning is necessary before firing. The warning is to be as clear as possible and is to include a direction to surrender and a clear warning that fire will be opened if the direction is not obeyed.

AREA OF OPERATIONS

8. Under no circumstances are you or your men to enter Spanish territory or Spanish territorial waters for the purposes connected with Operation 'Flavius', nor are you or your men to fire at any person on Spanish territory or Spanish territorial waters.

Thus, the SAS soldiers in Gibraltar were under strict guidelines as to the course of action they could follow. They had been thoroughly briefed and knew the type of people they were up against. With all the intelligence that had been gathered on the terrorists, the authorities believed they were certain of about five things. First, there would be an IRA attack during the changing of the guard ceremony on 8 March; second, the IRA team would use a large car bomb; third, the bomb would be triggered by remote control, ie a 'button job'; fourth, the IRA team would *not use* a blocking car to reserve a parking space in readiness for the car bomb because this would mean making two trips across the border; and finally, they knew that the IRA team was ruthless and thought they were armed.

All the above points were emphasised to the arresting SAS soldiers – 'A', 'B', 'C' and 'D'. However, they were wrong on three points: the terrorists were not armed, the car driven into Gibraltar and left in the square was a blocking car and didn't contain any explosives, and the bombers had decided to use a time bomb and not a radio-controlled device. Thus the SAS teams went onto the streets of Gibraltar believing the terrorists were carrying weapons and had the means to detonate the explosives electronically. In addition, the soldiers were briefed a second time in the early hours of Sunday morning, where it was impressed upon them again of the ruthlessness of the IRA team and the fact that they would use the weapons they were assumed to be carrying without hesitation if confronted, and they would also use the remote-control devices they were carrying.

Sunday 6 March was a beautiful sunny day, and all three terrorists, looking like any other tourists, crossed the border into Gibraltar. At 1450 hours they walked along the line of parked cars in the square and paused in front of their

Above: The intended target – the resident British Army band, which would have been annihilated.

white Renault 5. They were identified positively as being the three IRA terrorists. The two SAS teams were on the streets and were near the bombers. At 1455 hours, Colombo agreed to their arrest and handed over control to Soldier 'F' and the military. At that moment the three bombers turned and headed out of the square past Soldiers 'C' and 'D'. The SAS men then reported back to the Joint Operations Room but were told to hold back. Control was then passed back to the police.

At 1525 hours, the bombers returned to the car and then headed north towards the border. Soldier 'G' then dashed from the Joint Operations Room to make a quick examination of the car. He reported back to the commissioner that he had been unable to make a detailed survey of the car, but he believed, based on what he had seen (a suspicious aerial), that it could contain a bomb. Events now moved rapidly: at 1540 hours the Commissioner of Police handed over the power of arrest to the military. The terrorists reached the junction of Winston Churchill and Smith Dorrien Avenue. All four SAS soldiers began to close in on the IRA team. Soldier 'E' passed control to the two teams on the ground. At this point Savage split from the other two and

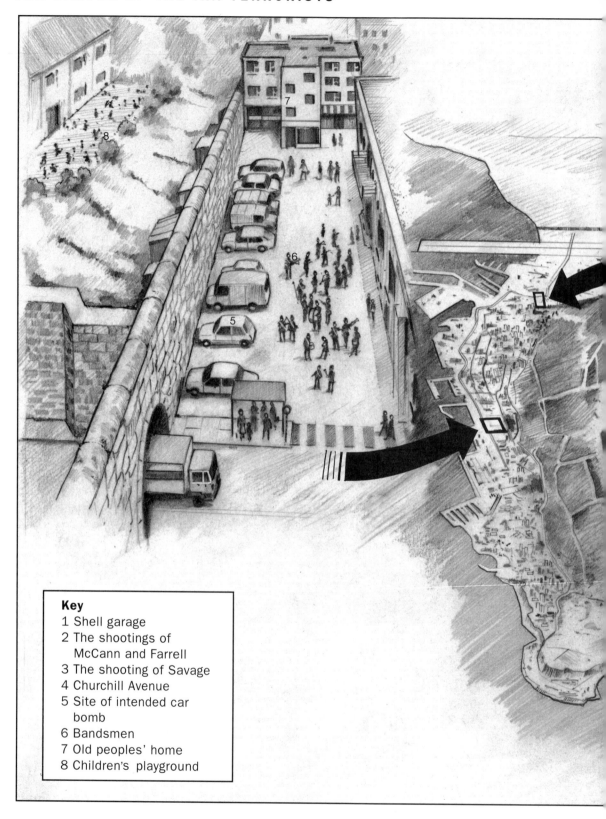

Key
1 Shell garage
2 The shootings of
   McCann and Farrell
3 The shooting of Savage
4 Churchill Avenue
5 Site of intended car
   bomb
6 Bandsmen
7 Old peoples' home
8 Children's playground

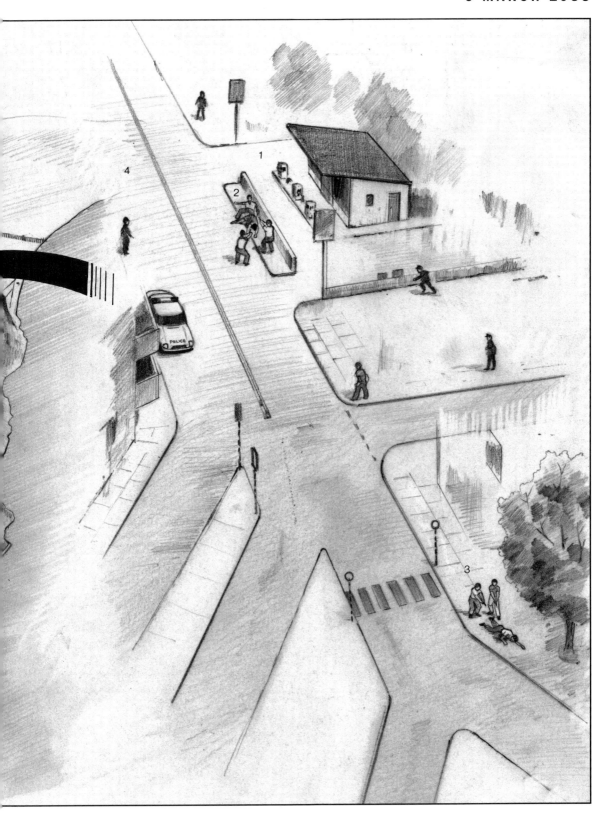

headed back towards the town centre, pursued by Soldiers 'C' and 'D'. McCann and Farrell continued walking towards the Shell garage on the right-hand side of Winston Churchill Avenue, closely followed by Soldiers 'A' and 'B'.

At 1600 hours, police headquarters radioed a police car to return to HQ at once because transport was needed to take the terrorists to jail after they had been arrested. The car switched on its siren and drove up Smith Dorrien. The siren startled the terrorists and began a sequence of events that was later described in detail by the SAS men. Soldier 'A' first engaged McCann:

'The look was alertness and very aware. At that stage, I was just about to shout a warning to stop and at the same time was drawing my pistol. I went to shout "stop" and I actually don't know if it came out. The look on McCann's face, the alertness, then all of a sudden the right elbow moving what I would call aggressively across the front of his body. I thought McCann was definitely going for a button. To me the whole worry was the bomb in the debussing area...I was drawing my weapon and fired at McCann one round into his back. I was about three metres away. We'd come up at a relatively brisk pace...Then I caught out of the corner of my eye a movement of Farrell who had a handbag under her left armpit, and grabbed at her bag. I thought she was going for the button and I shot Farrell in the back. I then engaged McCann with a further three rounds, one in the body and two in the head. He was falling all the time. His hands were away from his body...'

Soldier 'B' heard the sound of gunfire and saw Farrell draw her shoulder bag across her body. Uppermost in his mind was the remote-control device he thought she was carrying. He was also unaware if 'A' had been shot:

'So I opened fire. I drew my weapon as the shouting started and the firing began. It was all in a split second. She made a

movement to the right and I decided they were movements to detonate the device. I opened fire on Farrell and then I switched firing to McCann. I did not know if Soldier 'A' had been shot. I believed McCann to be an equal threat to myself, to the public and to my comrades.'

Savage was engaged by Soldiers 'C' and 'D', who moved in to arrest him when he turned and faced them, having been startled by the police siren. Soldier 'C' later testified at the inquest:

'Savage spun round very fast. I shouted "Stop". At the same time as I shouted, he went down to the right area of his jacket. At this stage, I had my weapon out to effect an arrest and I fired. I was about five to six feet away. I carried on firing until I was sure he'd gone down and was no longer a threat to initiate that device...I fired to the mass, to the body. He was full frontal because he had spun round. I could not take any more chances of effecting a physical arrest. I fired six rounds. Four went into the chest area, two went into the head. Savage spiralled down and then fell backwards.'

In a matter of seconds it was all over. The three terrorists lay dead, shot at close range by the SAS soldiers. Mairead Farrell was shot twice in the face and three times in the body, McCann twice in the head and twice in the body, while Savage was hit 15 times. They had all died extremely violent deaths; was it a case of overkill? Let's look at the facts.

The SAS soldiers all stated later at the inquest that the plan was for them to arrest the three suspects, and then they would disappear. At around 1530 hours they were informed by the explosives expert that the aerial on the parked car confirmed to him that the vehicle was 'suspect', which would have convinced the SAS soldiers that the terrorists were carrying remote-control devices. When they moved in for the arrest, both Soldier 'A' and 'B' said they saw Farrell and McCann make aggressive movements with their arms which made them believe they were going for the 'button' (an Army explosives expert stated at the inquest that it would have been possible for the three to detonate a bomb from the area where they were shot, testimony that was supported by an Army radio expert).

It was a similar situation for Soldiers 'C' and 'D', who were closing in on Savage. The terrorist made a sharp movement with his right arm to his jacket hip pocket, and the SAS soldiers fired because they believed he was going for the 'button'. The testimony of the soldiers reveals their SAS weapons training. Soldiers 'A' and 'D' stated that the terrorists would have to be incapacitated if they did not remain motionless after warnings had been shouted. When all three had failed to do so, they had opened fire to save lives, and, true to SAS drills, would remain firing until each target was no longer a threat. As Soldier 'E' stated: 'The intention from the moment that fire was opened was to kill him. That is standard and only by so doing could the threat be removed.'

The next day the British Foreign Secretary, Sir Geoffrey Howe, made a statement in the

Above: The price of failure. The funerals of the three IRA terrorists killed by the SAS at Gibraltar.

House of Commons concerning the incident which sought to explain the SAS's actions:

> 'When challenged, they [the terrorists] made movements which led the military personnel operating in support of the Gibraltar police to conclude that their own lives and the lives of others were under threat. In the light of this response, they were shot. Those killed were subsequently found not to have been carrying arms.'

The verdict of the inquest held into the shootings in September 1988 was that the three terrorists had been killed lawfully. In the final analysis, the SAS soldiers had acted according to their training and *on the information they had been supplied with at the briefing sessions*. There is little doubt that they would not have shot the three suspects if they had known that they were not armed and were not carrying detonation devices. Another of the SAS's battles was over.

THE GULF WAR

Dressed in Arab headdress, operating on foot and with Land Rovers, and armed to the teeth, SAS soldiers describe their daring Scud-busting exploits in the 1991 Gulf War.

O n 2 August 1990, around 100,000 Iraqi troops, led by six divisions of the elite Republican Guard, crossed the border into Kuwait. Within hours Kuwaiti resistance had effectively ended and Saddam Hussein, the Iraqi dictator, had achieved his goal of conquering the tiny oil-rich state. Political activity at the United Nations gave way to a military build-up in Saudi Arabia as it became clear the Iraqis could not be talked or coerced out of Kuwait. As UN troops poured into Saudi Arabia, American and British special forces units were also deployed, including elements of the Special Air Service (the story that SAS soldiers landed in Kuwait City on board a British Airways 747 jet during the Iraqi invasion is totally false).

In fact, the 1991 Gulf War was to witness the largest concentration of SAS troops on the ground since World War II. The Regiment was initially given a daunting task: the

An Iraqi tank on fire after being strafed by Allied ground-attack aircraft during Operation 'Desert Storm'. SAS teams called down many air strikes on enemy targets during the Gulf War.

rescue of British hostages. There were 800 British citizens being held in Kuwait itself, with a further 1000 in Iraq. In reality, this task would have been impossible. The hostages were dispersed to many military and strategically important locations, scattered around Saddam Hussein's domain as sacrificial lambs should Allied bombs start falling on his military installations and command centres. Though the SAS would have tried its utmost to rescue as many hostages as possible, there is no doubt that many would have been killed by Allied bombs, Iraqi guns, or even as a result of fleeing with members of the Regiment across the desert after they had been rescued, for what is possible to an SAS trooper is beyond the capabilities of an ordinary civilian. Fortunately this scenario didn't come about because the Iraqi dictator, in a rare moment of humanitarianism, let most of the hostages return to their countries of origin. This meant US and British special forces could concentrate their efforts on other tasks.

All special forces units in the Gulf were controlled by the Allied Special Operations Command of Central Command (SOCCENT). In August 1990, D and G Squadrons, 22 SAS, were in the Gulf region honing their desert warfare skills. One of those SAS soldiers remembers the rapid build-up in Saudi Arabia:

'Our Hercules touched down just before sunset, rattling past neatly parked groups of fighter aircraft which lined the apron of Riyadh air base. Compared to us they looked the "business", but from experience I knew never to judge a book by its cover. Our aged boneshaker taxied to a halt and the fuselage began to fill with engine fumes. I'm sure the RAF leak them deliberately into the cabin to send passengers to sleep. Fortunately, the load master noticed our situation and lowered the rear ramp before we chocked to death. A gush of fresh Arabian air brushed past our faces as we shuffled off the aircraft.

'We had been operating in Oman with a batch of new four-wheel drive vehicles called Light Strike Vehicles, which were designed specifically for rough terrain. We

had spent weeks putting them through a series of punishing tests. They were good, though the suspension couldn't survive a drop from a Chinook helicopter from an altitude of 100m, which we discovered when one was accidentally dropped. Still, there isn't much kit that can survive that sort of treatment. We were thoroughly acclimatised by the time we touched down in Saudi, though none of us were prepared for the piss-poor weather we would encounter later on operations.

'So there we were, a motley crew with bergens and weapons walking across the tarmac to a group of waiting trucks. Around us, an army of multinational air force personnel worked feverishly on their aircraft. We didn't know what the high command had in store for us, so all we could do was train for any likely operation that might crop up. By late December 1990, the majority of the Regiment had been deployed to the Gulf, including some blokes from R Squadron, the reserve. However, because no specific role had been assigned to us, patience began to wear a little thin.'

Ultimately, the UK special forces group in the Gulf numbered 700 men, including elements of the Special Boat Squadron (SBS) and RAF special forces aircrew. The SAS contingent comprised some 300 men: A, B and D Squadrons and 15 men from R Squadron (G Squadron was not used in the end). The RAF Special Forces Flight operated CH-47 Chinook helicopters in support of SAS operations:

'The Chinooks assigned to SF (special forces) operations were repainted in a camouflage scheme designed for night operations. The new colour was ordered after the helicopter aircrews became concerned that the original desert pink colour might be picked up by any Iraqi forces operating night vision equipment. As a result, black paint was used to tone down the Chinook's profile. Compared to the dull desert colour schemes of other

Above: An SAS team photographed in Oman shortly before being deployed to operate behind the lines in Iraq. Note the handles taped to the MP5s.

aircraft, the RAF's SF flight gave the appearance of being scruffy and dirty. Nevertheless, the colour was a success and it blended in with the local terrain. Mind you, a lot of the lads thought that it looked like a graffiti gang had gone mad with a few spray cans.'

The relationship that grew up between the soldiers of the Regiment and the the RAF's No 7 Special Forces Squadron during the Gulf conflict was a close one. The Chinooks played a major role in the behind-the-lines operations under-taken by the SAS in the war. A member of the Regiment involved in an operation in Iraq remembers the sterling work carried out by the men of No 7 Squadron:

'The throb of the twin-tandem rotors filled the fuselage as the Chinook hugged the contours of the ground in its efforts to avoid enemy radar. Inside the aircraft the team was cramped to say the least, as the RAF boys had put in this fucking great big rubber bag full of extra aviation fuel to make sure we had the range to get to the target. We checked our weapons and kit, talk was almost impossible in the deafening noise, and anyway the cabin was in darkness. Then came the signal to ready ourselves for debussing. We arrived at the location just before midnight – we had four hours on the ground to locate and confirm that an Iraqi radar station that had been identified by aerial photographs was real and not a decoy. The Iraqis had deployed a number of German-made dummy radar stations just before hostilities started, and it was one of the jobs of the special forces to go in and confirm targets before they were subjected to Allied bombing raids.

'Once on the ground we had major problems finding the target, as we were continually lashed by freezing winds. I remember saying to myself, "I thought this was the bloody desert, not the Falklands". Anyway, our visibility was reduced to almost zero and our strength was being sapped rapidly as we tried to battle against the wind. Struggling on, we eventually found the radar station and confirmed it was for real.

'Though we were thankful the trip hadn't been wasted, I for one was very apprehensive that we wouldn't make it back to the rendezvous on time. In fact, we were an hour behind schedule when we got back. The boss radioed our position and requested evacuation. I thought we would have to spend the night on the ground because of the bad weather, but then we heard the dull throb of the Chinook as it swooped in to land. Fucking champion. However, by this time we were being lashed by both wind and sleet, and it was almost impossible for us to see each other. The boss ordered us to link arms as the RAF crewman flashed an orange light to guide us through the storm and beneath the down-draft of the rotors. It was a relieved team that sat in the comparative comfort of the Chinook as it made its way back to Allied lines.'

Several days later the same aircraft, again waiting for an SAS team, ran out of luck when it landed in a minefield behind enemy lines. It was forced to lift off immediately, having had one of its rear wheels blown off and its fuselage pitted with fragmentation holes. Despite the condition of the aircraft, though, the pilot made it back to friendly lines.

Ironically, despite the rapid build-up of British and American special forces in the Gulf,

no one knew what to do with them, apart from using them in penny-packet operations. The situation wasn't helped by the attitude of the Allied supreme commander, General Norman Schwarzkopf, who, because of his bad experiences with special forces units in Vietnam, was suspicious of elite units.

'At first Norman Schwarzkopf had opposed the idea of deploying them [special forces] behind enemy lines, on the grounds that there was no task which could not be carried out by the Allies' overwhelming air power or, later, by the conventional armoured forces. I myself was not prepared to recommend special operations unless two conditions were fulfilled: one was that there must be a real, worthwhile role for the SAS to perform, and the other that we must have some means of extricating our men in an emergency.'

The above words are those of General Peter de la Billière, the British commander in the Gulf. He had served with the SAS and had risen to eventually command the entire SAS Group. De la Billière persuaded Schwarzkopf that the special forces should be given a chance to prove themselves, but to do what? The answer came on 18 January 1991, when the first Scud surface-to-surface (SSM) missile was launched by Iraq against Israel in an attempt to bring the Jewish state into the war. The Scud is an extremely basic weapon: a solid-fuel rocket with a warhead on top, albeit one that can contain chemical or biological agents, which is pointed in the general direction of the target and is fired. It can be fired from fixed rocket sites or from mobile launchers. Ironically, the Scud could have been the most lethal weapon of the whole conflict. If Israel had been dragged into the war the coalition, containing as it did Arab nations, would have probably fallen apart, and there would have been a real possibility of Saudi Arabia expelling Western forces from its soil.

Right: A special forces Chinook helicopter, several of which supported SAS operations in the Gulf.

Above : The Longline Light Strike Vehicle, as used by the SAS for reconnaissance in the Gulf.

Therefore, special forces units were tasked with hunting down the mobile launchers and fixed sites and either destroying them themselves or calling in air strikes to do the job.

On 19 January the SAS was rushed to its Forward Operating Base (FOB), which was one day's drive away from the western Iraqi border. The SAS and American special forces, for it was very much a joint effort, had two main tasks: the tracking down of mobile and static Scuds, and

the destruction of the concealed Iraqi communications links. Saddam Hussein had built up these links over a number of years. Ironically, he had done so with the help of Western defence and intelligence agencies, who had impressed upon him the need for secure and robust communications links throughout the country. They consisted in the main of microwave links maintained by a series of communications towers, and fibre optic cables buried under the ground.

To battle the Scuds, the SAS employed two methods: the mounting of static road watch patrols, and mobile fighting columns. The road watches were in the true SAS tradition, ie they were high risk and extremely daring! Teams of eight men were inserted by helicopter up to 300km behind enemy lines, where they established covert observation posts and literally watched the road for enemy activity. If they saw any worthwhile targets, they radioed headquarters to order an air strike. The men had no transport apart from their feet, and if compromised they had only their own resources and skills to make it back to friendly lines.

The fighting columns usually consisted of around 12 heavily armed Land Rover vehicles, which formed hunter-killer groups. They operated mostly in the 'Scud Box', an area of land near the border with Jordan. Comprising some 500 square kilometres of territory, it included the Baghdad-Amman road and was usually filled with travelling Bedouins, civilian traffic and a sizeable enemy military presence. Initially, it had been anticipated that Light Strike Vehicles (LSVs) would be extensively used, though events were to prove otherwise:

'The four two-man LSVs ferried across from Oman were considered ideal for cross-border raids. They had many clever design features, including armoured seats and self-sealing fuel tanks to counter fragmentation damage. But as the Gulf situated escalated, it became clear that instead of operating on a limited scale using the two strike vehicles, the Regiment would be called upon to mount much bigger vehicle-based operations. In the event, LSVs were used by SAS patrols to monitor Iraqi movements, but they didn't cross the border into enemy territory.

'A fleet of new Land Rovers arrived for us from the UK, all stripped down for desert operations and decorated with a host of weapon mounts and additional fittings, including Southdown Protection Systems, which stopped the transmission systems from being damaged on rocks.'

The road watch patrols were conducted by B Squadron along three highways in the Euphrates Valley. There were three patrols in total, called the North, Central and South road watches. Right from the start it was apparent to the commander of the South road watch that his position was untenable and so he abandoned it and returned to base (he was lucky enough to have helicopter evacuation). The Central watch was just as precarious, so its commander also had no choice but to evacuate his team, though not before he had called down an air strike on two enemy mobile radar systems that were positioned close by. The SAS soldiers then left the area at speed, and began an epic 220km journey over four extremely cold nights before making it back to Saudi Arabia.

The story of the North watch north is one of heroism and tragedy which sums up much of what the SAS is all about. Dropped 300km from friendly lines, the men quickly settled down to a routine of keeping watch, sleeping and carrying out minor duties to keep their minds active. No one thought about their precarious position much, and if they did it was with that typical sang-froid that is the hallmark of the Regiment's soldiers. On the second day an Iraqi convoy appeared and established itself near by, though it would be more accurate to say almost on top of the SAS soldiers. When it had stopped and set itself up, the British soldiers were perturbed to discover that it was a mobile anti-aircraft battery, complete with a fearsome array of anti-aircraft guns. Very soon the inevitable happened: the SAS men were compromised, though not by Iraqi soldiers but by a group of curious civilians who were attached to the enemy convoy. The SAS men did the only sensible thing: they ran like hell. Heavily laden with bergens, they bugged out without further ado. They quickly attracted the sort of attention all soldiers wish to avoid, and very soon a hail of bullets was being directed at them. The Iraqi anti-aircraft guns were also brought to bear, and one SAS trooper had his bergen literally ripped to shreds by machine-gun fire. Ditching their backpacks, the SAS soldiers increased the speed of their flight.

Thinking quickly, they headed in the general direction of the Syrian border, eight men on a desperate venture. Behind them the countryside was alive with soldiers as the Iraqis

Key
1 SAS Land Rovers
2 Mobile Scud launchers
3 Iraqi BMP infantry
   fighting vehicles
4 Iraqi BRDM patrol
   vehicles
5 Iraqi trucks
6 Iraqi machine guns

desperately hunted for the unknown enemy troops who had been in their midst. The Arabian desert is an inhospitable place at the best of times, but in January 1991 the weather conditions were particularly severe. The area was being treated to a potentially lethal cocktail of

rain, sleet, wind and snow, and these were the conditions the SAS soldiers had to battle against in their efforts to escape death or capture. The group split up to increase its overall chances of evasion. With few supplies and the enemy at their heels, the men were forced to maintain a cruel pace. Inevitably, they began to falter. One, Sergeant Vince Phillips, got separated from his group in the driving sleet and died of exhaustion and hypothermia in the Iraqi hills. Another member of his three-man group was surrounded by enemy soldiers and forced to surrender. The

Above: Peter de la Billière (left), an SAS veteran who commanded British forces in the Gulf.

third, Corporal 'Z', displayed the sort of tenacity and cunning that is the stuff of screen super heroes. Walking day and night, avoiding all contact with any other humans, taking refreshment where he found it, he covered 200km on foot and made it to the Syrian border. His achievement is all the more remarkable because for the last 48 hours of his journey he was without water. Such is the calibre of men who wear the winged dagger badge.

The other five initially had better luck. They reached the town of Al Qaim, near the Jordanian border, before being bumped by a group of Iraqi soldiers. This heralded a series of heavy gun battles as the SAS men, heavily outnumbered, held the enemy at bay with controlled, accurate fire. But they couldn't

Left: Another Iraqi target is destroyed, courtesy of Britain's Special Air Service Regiment.

had been pushed beyond their limits, but with dogged determination they had kept going. But now, beset by the enemy and the terrible weather, their systems were giving out. The last two, unbelievably, continued to head for sanctuary, but fate was to be cruel. One of them, Lance-Corporal Lane, was almost unconscious as his companion got him inside a cabin. But to no avail: Lane died of hypothermia shortly after. His companion attempted to escape but was captured. Thus ended the road watch venture, a plan that was perhaps a little too audacious. But for the Regiment the war was not over: the fighting columns were about to begin.

The first crossed the Saudi border on 20 January, a line of heavily armed vehicles from A Squadron. Though they mounted a variety of weapons, one of the most valued pieces of kit was the US-made Magellan Global Positioning System (GPS) receivers carried by the men:

'Before the war we had been exercising and using the GPS with great results. In the Gulf smaller sets were available, and their accuracy was astonishing. Though they were expensive, for us the GPS receivers were among the best items of kit purchased by the Ministry of Defence. They were brilliant for coordinating rendezvous sites and directing air strikes.'

Some of the dress worn by SAS soldiers in the Gulf War differed little from that worn 50 years earlier by their predecessors in the North African desert:

'*Shemaghs*, an Arab headdress, was the order of the day. We looked a bit like a bunch of *Lawrence of Arabia* stand-ins, but they kept the sand and dust out of our faces and that was all that mattered. By mid-January 1991, we were across the border and operating in the Iraqi desert, experiencing the cold nights and savage winds. Desert combats were worn, but on their own were no match for the terrible

shake off the Iraqis, despite inflicting heavy casualties on them. Trooper Robert Consiglio, covering the withdrawal, was hit and killed (the loss of this Swiss-born soldier was keenly felt; he was reckoned to be one of the fittest members of the Regiment). Two others were captured soon after. The SAS soldiers were men whose bodies conditions. So, Goretex jackets, climbing jumpers, gloves, arctic smocks and woolly hats were pulled out of our bergens for

warmth. Forget the idea of a smartly dressed patrol, we looked like a bunch of unshaven gypsies.

'Some teams wore chest webbing and a belt order, while others just wore a heavy belt order, which carried all the

Below: US Special Forces personnel enter Kuwait City in a Chenworth Fast Attack Vehicle.

operational equipment that had been drawn up for desert warfare: emergency food, survival kit, binoculars, compass, a GPS receiver (for the team leader), water bottles, NBC med-pack of atropine, ammunition, white phosphorus grenades,

charge packs and and as many Claymore mines as we could carry.'

The men had been thoroughly prepared for encountering Scuds:

> 'Our months of waiting to move into Iraq had included detailed intelligence briefings about Iraqi Scuds, how to identify them, how to spot traces of a Scud site and, most important of all, how to destroy the fucking big mobile rocket platforms.'

Another two columns, from D Squadron, also entered Iraqi territory to hunt for Scuds. They were not to be disappointed. Nine days after crossing the border, an SAS column came across a camouflaged fixed Scud site which was preparing to launch a salvo of missiles against Israel. The SAS commander quickly radioed for an air strike. Minutes later, American F-15 Eagles streaked across the sky, locked onto their target and destroyed the missile site with their ordnance. The special forces were beginning to pay back the faith that had been put in them.

It wasn't all one-way traffic, though. The SAS had to be vigilant. The vehicles were always arranged in defensive circles during rest and maintenance periods – a sort of late twentieth-century wagon train, except the Indians in this case were Iraqi soldiers. One such 'Indian' raid took place on the same day as another SAS column was ordering the strike on the fixed missile battery. A group of Iraqi vehicles stumbled across an SAS column and started to fire at it with small arms and heavy machine guns. The SAS soldiers, whose reflexes are never slow, almost instantaneously returned fire and a savage firefight ensued. As is often the case in such encounters, the side with the strongest nerves and the steadiest trigger fingers often comes out on top. And so it was. The Iraqis were beaten off, losing 10 dead and three vehicles.

The SAS's favourite hunting ground was Wadi Amij, near the town of Ar Rutbah, which was nicknamed 'Scud Alley'. On 3 February 1991, a fighting column from D Squadron was operating in the 'Alley' when it spotted an Iraqi Scud convoy of 14 vehicles. The SAS

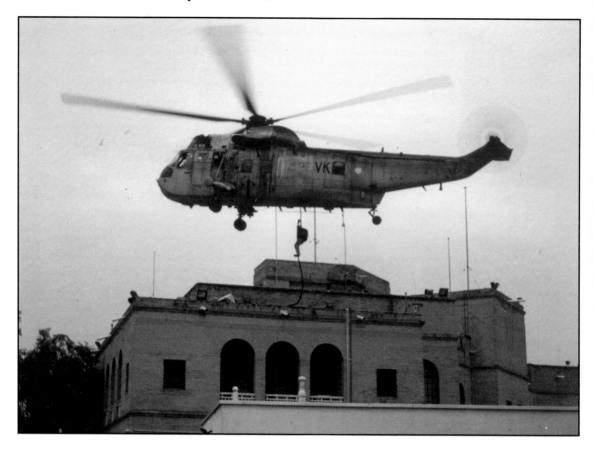

Above: A Sea King lands SBS men on the roof of the British Embassy in Kuwait City, February 1991.

commander called up an air strike and the troopers watched as American A-10s and F-15s raked the enemy column with rockets and bombs. A trailer and its Scud took a direct hit, the vehicle being thrown into the air in a red fireball of burning explosives and petrol. A truck was flipped onto its side and an armoured personnel carrier was riddled with holes, its occupants killed as shrapnel tore through their bodies. But amidst the death and destruction it became apparent that the aircraft had not done the whole job: there were still some vehicles intact. The SAS column therefore opened up with its Milan anti-tank missiles. The rockets streaked across the flat terrain and began to find their targets. But the Iraqis spotted their adversaries and returned fire with their small arms and anti-aircraft guns. The latter's rounds kicked up sand and earth around the SAS jeeps as

the battle intensified. Rather than risk heavy casualties, the SAS commander gave the order for his vehicles to pull back, while at the same time radioing for another air strike. He knew the Iraqi column was like a beached whale – it wasn't going anywhere after the pounding it had taken. A few minutes later, as the SAS vehicles headed away, the men heard the satisfying thump and crump of aircraft bombs hitting the enemy column for a second time. Intelligence gathered later revealed that all the Iraqi vehicles had been destroyed.

Not all encounters between Iraqi Scud convoys and the SAS occurred in 'Scud Alley'. The following account is told by a member of one of the Regiment's fighting columns, who at the time was returning to the Saudi border:

'After three days we had failed to locate the site we were looking for and had problems raising our FOB. We used a burst form of transmission which basically stores your message then transmits it at speed so the enemy can't get a fix on you. Therefore, the decision was taken to leave "Scud Alley" and head back towards the Allied border. Our Land Rovers were fitted with Milans, machine guns and Mark 19 automatic grenade launchers. The Milan is a fucking good piece of kit: accurate, reliable and has excellent armour penetration capabilities. It also has an effective range of 2000m, which means you don't have to get too close to the opposition to score a direct hit. The Land Rovers didn't have Milan mounts as such. However, good old SAS ingenuity came into its own. We used a home-made bracket improvised from wood and para-cord and strapped to the roll bar.

'As we moved through the barren, flat desert we spotted a number of vehicles ahead of us. We pulled over and observed them with our scopes and binoculars. Bingo! They were Iraqi military transporters, so the boss ordered us to head towards them. When we were within 600m we could identify the target – a Scud launcher and a missile trailer. The Iraqis were in the process of camouflaging the vehicles and had forgotten to post any sentries. Big mistake.

'We quickly held a briefing and decided to divide our firepower between the two targets. A hand signal from the boss would begin the attack. We edged forward and the signal was given. The next moment several Milan missiles streaked across the desert and slammed into the enemy vehicles. A fireball engulfed the Iraqis as explosives combined with fuel to form a lethal cocktail. And then it was all over. Elation. We roared off at full speed, our minds racing with thoughts of what the Iraqi commander would do; we are trained to think like the enemy so you can take effective evasive action. We were on top of the world, but we had no time to gloat. We had to get away from the area as fast as possible, re-group and arrange a rendezvous with our supply vehicles.

'Later in the war some American A-10 aircraft strafed some British Army vehicles by mistake, killing nine soldiers. After this incident one of our SOPs was to lay out a Union Jack flag, pegged out with stones, on the ground whenever we stopped so it could be seen by aircraft overhead (there were no enemy aircraft operating by this stage of the war).'

Occasionally, SAS fighting columns would be reinforced with additional troops flown in by helicopter. A member of one such 12-man team remembers an operation against Iraqi Scuds that took place in January:

'The Regiment did well against Hussein's Scuds, but it wasn't all plain sailing. I remember there was a lot of fierce firefights between our "mobiles" and enemy troops. The sector of Iraq assigned to the SAS was described by our men as being "toppers with targets", on account of the area being a prime location for the huge rocket sites and mobile launchers. In January, one of our mobile columns had identified a Scud position and called down an air strike on it. The immediate area was saturated with enemy troops, which meant our team legged it quickly after checking the damage done by the F15s. While they were reporting back to Saudi, however, they were informed that one of the launchers was still intact.

'In a hastily drawn-up plan we were flown in by helicopter to rendezvous with the mobile column, which was going to have another crack. We were then given an on-the-ground briefing for the attack on the launcher site. The boss decided to try and lure the Iraqis from their defended positions by using "come ons": small charges planted roughly one kilometre from their camp. Hopefully they would venture forth to investigate, leaving us to destroy their site while their minds were on other things. We didn't fancy taking on the Iraqis where they were, as they had set up a host of machine-gun nests and they

165

might have had heavier stuff, such as artillery, which we couldn't see.

'The heliborne team was split into two and deployed on the flanks. It was bloody freezing as dawn broke over the arid terrain, and no one spoke a word as we waited for the charges to detonate. I remember casting a quick glance at the other guys. They were wrapped up like it was the arctic. Then we heard the thump, thump of the charges going off one by one. Then the Iraqis started to fire, not aimed shots but wild bursts that sprayed everywhere. They weren't going to leave the safety of their camp. Oh well, if Mohammed won't come to the mountain...

'Now it was our turn. The plan was for the main force of Land Rovers to conduct the main attack against the Scud site, while the Milans on the flanks would concentrate on the launchers. A steady and well-aimed stream of SAS GPMG and Browning .5in rounds poured into the Iraqi position as the camp began to catch fire. I didn't know what was burning, but it made an excellent point of reference for all the gunners. Then the Milans opened up, the missiles racing across the ground and slamming into their targets. A fireball erupted as a fuel tanker was hit. The launchers disappeared in a pall of smoke, and Iraqi soldiers began to flee their positions, only to be cut down by our withering fire.

'Then there was silence, interspersed by the sound of ammunition being ignited by the flames or fuel exploding in vehicles. The Scuds site was now totally immobilised. The commander quickly surveyed the scene and then gave the order to bug out. We left the area at speed and reported in our position and direction. As the sun started to climb into the desert sky, we congratulated ourselves on a job well done,'

The SAS also continued hitting enemy communications systems. After one such attack, on 21 February, a column from A Squadron was involved in running battles with an Iraqi force. The British soldiers managed to beat off their

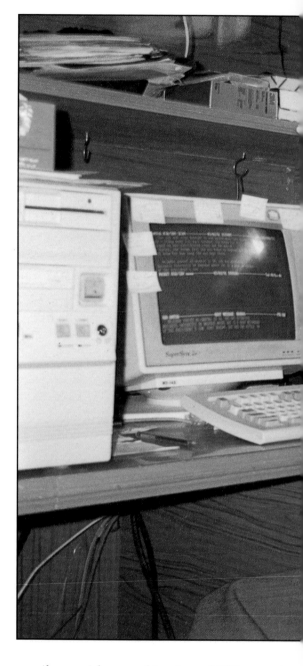

assailants with a combination of Milans and Browning machine guns, but an SAS motorcyclist, Lance-Corporal David Denbury, was mortally wounded. Nevertheless, the Regiment made a sizeable contribution to the war against Saddam Hussein's communications systems.

A little-known part of the SAS campaign during the Gulf War concerned the collation of intelligence gained from Kuwaiti sources. In

Above: 'Mohammed', who risked his life to transmit messages to the Allies from Kuwait City.

Riyadh, several SAS soldiers worked alongside US Special Forces intelligence personnel to produce detailed information concerning Iraqi troop strengths in Kuwait. The operation was manned by three SAS linguists, who worked with three American counterparts. Their initial task was to locate and secure a source of regular and reliable information inside Kuwait City that could provide intelligence about the enemy to

contribute towards the liberation of the city. In its efforts, the SAS struck gold:

'The SAS team targeted radio hams, and through a "third player" in Geneva were able to make contact with "Mohammed", a school teacher and computer expert who lived in Kuwait City and who had transmitted around the globe as a radio ham for 10 years. Elements of the Kuwaiti resistance were supplying information via Sat-Com [satellite communications], but the latter relied on high-frequency transmissions and the Iraqis were often able to identify the source of the sets and arrest their users.

'The kit used by "Mohammed" emitted a low pulse which was much more difficult to pinpoint. To add to his security he only operated at certain times of the day from his basement cellar, where he had three computer terminals linked to his radio transmitter, which he used to send messages straight to western Europe. He had a small generator outside the house which he used to boost the two huge industrial batteries that formed his power source. His information was spot on most of the time. One of our guys and an American visited him three days after the war had ended to thank him personally on behalf of all the Allied special forces. He was a very brave person.'

This, then, was the SAS in the 1991 Gulf War, undertaking intelligence gathering duties and hunting down Scud missiles to prevent Israel entering the war. What, in the final analysis, did the Regiment achieve? Perhaps the final verdict should belong to Schwarzkopf himself:

'I wish to officially commend the 22nd Special Air Service (SAS) Regiment for their totally outstanding performance of military operations during Operation Desert Storm...The performance of the 22nd Special Air Service (SAS) Regiment during Operation Desert Storm was in the highest traditions of the professional military service and in keeping with the proud history and tradition that has been established by that regiment.'

Right: One tragedy the SAS couldn't prevent – the oil fields set alight by retreating Iraqi forces.

THE FUTURE

SAS soldiers talk candidly about the tasks and difficulties the Regiment will face in the future, such as the battle against international drug gangs, and also the problems of resources and manpower that may adversely affect the world's most highly trained military unit.

On the face of it, the main wartime role of the SAS has disappeared. Up to the end of the 1980s, the Regiment was heavily involved in training for operations behind the lines in eastern Europe and the Soviet Union in the event of a military confrontation between the Warsaw Pact and NATO. However, with the collapse of the Soviet bloc and its fragmentation into a number of non-aligned states, the threat from the east has largely gone. The 'new world order' talked of by ex-president of the United States George Bush has theoretically made redundant such units as the SAS. Unfortunately, this 'new world order', far from ushering in a period of international peace and prosperity, has created uncertainty and de-stabilisation throughout many areas of the world. As a result, the SAS is needed more than ever. But to do what? One of the main priorities of the Regiment now is fighting international terrorism.

Practising parachute insertion techniques. SAS soldiers are multi-skilled operatives, but will future demands made on the Regiment result in less time for training?

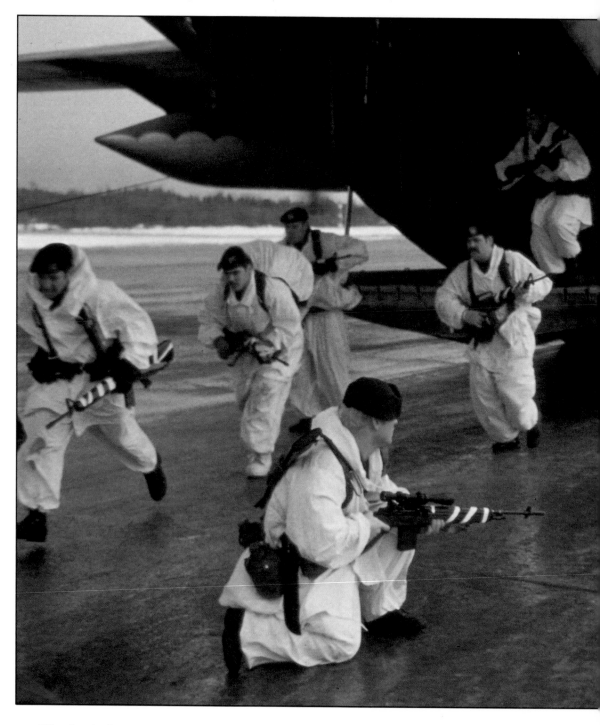

The fact is that European and US counter-terrorist units are stretched to the limit, a situation not helped by the current trend to cut back on defence spending in the West as a result of the so-called 'peace dividend' (the facile assumption that now the Warsaw Pact has gone, all threat of conflict in the world has disappeared; meanwhile, the 1991 Gulf War witnessed the largest wartime deployment of Western forces since the Korean War):

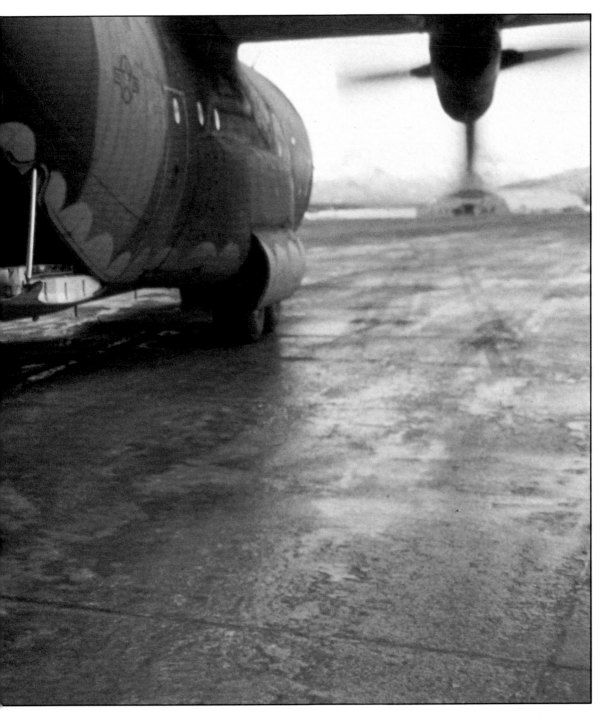

'The weekly intelligence briefing at Stirling Lines highlights the current activities of leading international terror groups. There are currently more than 300 active terrorist cells operating worldwide,

Above: The SAS conducts cross-training with many units, such as these US Special Forces.

hawking violence and death as their trademark. In the area of Counter

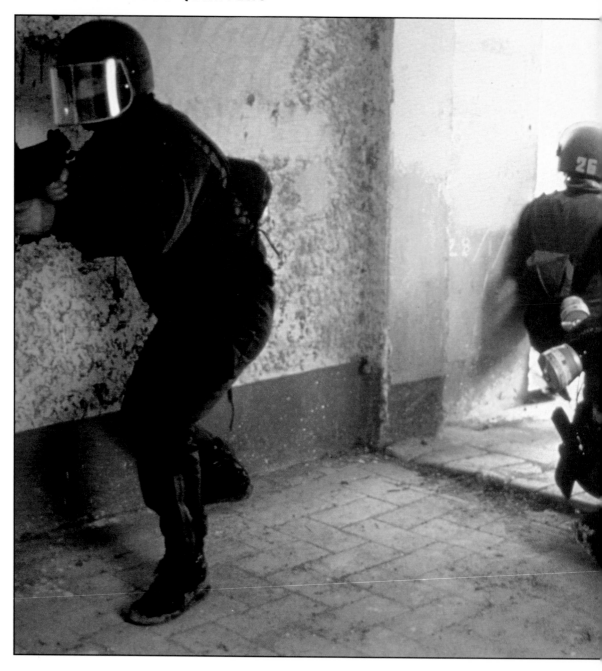

Revolutionary Warfare (CRW), the Regiment works alongside German, French, Spanish and American units, sharing ideas and concepts.'

The international nature of terrorism has resulted in close cooperation between the organisations set up to fight it. A cursory look at current terrorist activity does not make happy reading. In Germany, the Red Army Faction has been in existence since the late 1960s. Although now tiny due to a determined campaign against it by the police, it is still active. In 1989, for example, it assassinated the chairman of the Deutsche Bank, Alfred Herrhausen, using a remote-controlled bomb. In Italy, the Red

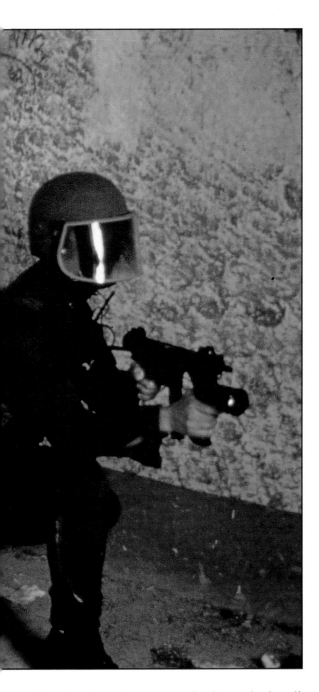

Left: The SAS has close links with many Western counter-terrorist units. These men are from NOCS.

Since the 1970s, national governments in Europe have established a number of dedicated counter-terrorist units. In Germany, *Grenzschutzgruppe 9 (GSG 9)* was set up after the 1972 Munich Olympics; in Italy, *Nucleo Operativo Centrale di Sicurezza (NOCS)* was trained in counter-terrorist tactics by the SAS; France established the counter-terrorist unit *Groupement d'Intervention de la Gendarmerie Nationale (GIGN)*; and in the United States Delta Force was created in 1977 following GSG 9's successful operation at Mogadishu. All these groups, including the SAS, undertake frequent cross-training with each other, resulting in a constant interchange of information about specialist weapons, equipment and tactics. However, cross-training has presented a number of problems to the Regiment:

'The SAS is facing a major problem with regard to meeting growing demands with fewer resources. What people don't realise is that the Regiment is quite small. Its "badged" men – those who have passed Selection and Continuation – number around 350 men. Support units of vital tradesmen such as medics and signallers serve alongside the Regiment and wear the beige beret with their own cap badge, but it is the "badged" men who form the Sabre Squadrons. Each SAS trooper can serve up to eight months out of every year "deployed" away from Hereford on operational duties and training commitments. In 1992, for example, one trooper spent just seven weeks out of the whole year at Stirling Lines.

'To boost the available manpower to meet the growing demands, it has been proposed that the Royal Marines Special Boat Squadron (SBS) join forces with the SAS, thus reducing overheads and centralising the skills of both formations. However, the merger idea was abandoned in early 1990 after fierce lobbying by the Royal Marines to keep their "swimmer

Brigades, though now greatly diminished, still have a number of active cells, and in Spain the Basque group ETA continues its terror campaign to win self-determination for the Basque homeland. In addition, the easing of border controls as a result of the strengthening of the European Community has made it easy for terrorist groups to transport arms across the continent.

canoeists" within the Corps, and thus retain its beach reconnaissance capacity for amphibious landings. For the moment it appears that the two formations will remain separate, but in the current climate of financial restraints the prospect of merger is by no means remote, and in 1994 there will be the first joint SAS/SBS Selection course. If it is successful, it will herald the closure of the SBS's training base at Portland, Dorset.

'Despite the uncertainty with regards to organisational changes, some things don't change. There will always be the fight against the IRA, for example. At the same time, the Regiment always trains for the unexpected, such as a Gulf War scenario or a hostage-rescue situation.'

In a world of change one thing is certain: there will not be peace in the short term in Northern Ireland. Both the British and Irish governments have tried hard to bring about a peaceful solution to the conflict, most notably the Anglo-Irish agreement of November 1985, which gave the Irish Republic a direct role in Northern Ireland affairs for the first time. The British know that the likelihood of defeating the IRA is remote, but they hope the Provos will eventually lose support as the lot of Catholics in the Province is improved, which, combined with a general war-weariness, will result in a de facto ceasefire. To date, however, this scenario shows no sign of happening.

This being the case, the SAS continues its war against the terrorists. For its part the IRA has, since the 1970s, become ever more proficient and deadly. Sophisticated weapons were supplied to the Provisionals from the United States and the Middle East in the 1980s, for example, and the money raised for the Republican cause has meant that IRA terrorists have received the very best with regards to training and equipment. Libyan arms and American money, plus cash raised through extortion, has resulted in the IRA becoming a 'slick' organisation, one which has become expert at using violence as an instrument to further its aims, and the war has spread beyond Ulster's shores. In

1989, for example, the IRA killed 10 Royal Marines at Deal, Kent, and shot an RAF corporal and his six-month-old child in Germany; in 1990, the Tory MP Ian Gow was killed by a car bomb and the London stock exchange was bombed; in 1991, there was a bombing campaign in London and the Prime Minister's home in Downing Street was mortar bombed; in 1992 more bombs went off in London; and in the latest outrage, in April 1993, the Bishop's Gate area of the City of London was wrecked by IRA explosives.

The SAS continues to fight back in the deadly cat-and-mouse game. Since 1990 it has killed a number of IRA terrorists in numerous ambushes: Martin Corrigan, killed in Armagh in April 1990 while attempting to murder an Army reservist; Desmond Grew, nicknamed the 'Widow Maker', shot at Loughall in October 1990 while moving a consignment of Kalashnikov rifles; Alexander Patterson, a man responsible for the deaths of numerous civilians, including women and children, killed in November 1990 while firing on the house of a UDR reservist in Strabane; Peter Ryan, shot by the SAS in June 1991 in Coagh while on his way to murder someone; and Kevin Barry O'Donnell, Sean O'Farrell, Patrick Vincent and Peter Clancy, all ambushed in Clonoe, Coalisland, after machine gunning a police station. Though there is only troop operating in the Province – Ulster Troop – the SAS's commitment in Northern Ireland shows no sign of ending, a fact that will further tax the Regiment's resources.

The SAS is one of the best special forces units in the world. This fact is not lost on the allies and friends of Great Britain, who often request SAS advice on a host of matters. As a result, there has been an increase in 'advisory' roles undertaken by SAS soldiers:

'There is a long list of security tasks, as well as the increasing requirement for training teams. The latter provide military instruction to "friendly forces" in the Middle East and elsewhere, and they keep the Regiment's calendar fully booked. At any one time there are SAS advisors in

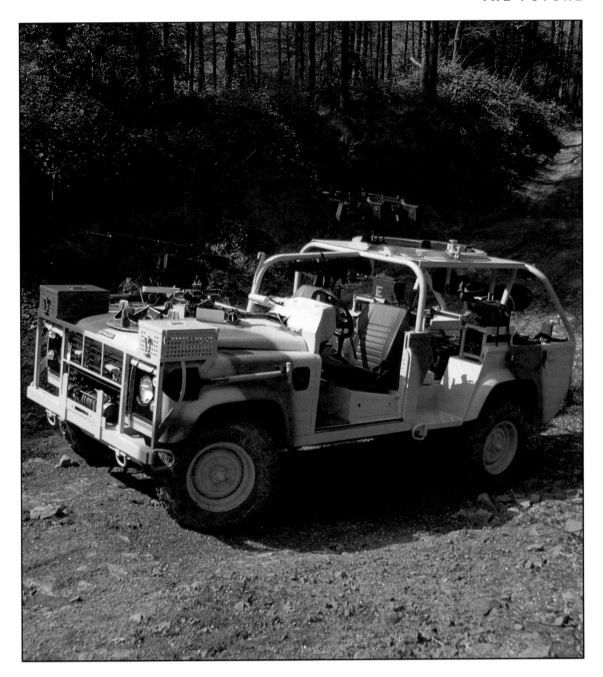

Above: The Land Rover SOV, one of the new vehicles currently entering service with the SAS.

Ulster, Belize, Brunei, the USA and the Middle East. Then there are the one-off jobs that crop up. In one month, for example, there were some of our blokes testing the defences of the Falklands and Ascension Island, as well as checking the security of two key military locations in the UK and preparing for an exercise in Gibraltar.

'Because of the pressure on manpower, many of these "jobs" are filled by men from .R Squadron, the reserve squadron which is based at Hereford. Unlike the other two Territorial Army units, 21 and

177

23 SAS, the men who serve in .R Squadron must all have previous military service. Indeed, they attend the same Selection courses as the regulars. Because of this they are all highly regarded.'

Special forces traditionally employ sophisticated equipment in their operations. This being the case, the SAS has an Operations Research Wing that continually tests and evaluates new equipment and weapons for the Regiment.

Transportation, for example, has always been an important part of SAS operations:

Below: A vulnerable target – a North Sea oil rig. The SAS is now responsible for their safety.

'A development unit is constantly working on new concepts and methods of operation for the Mobility, Air, Mountain and Boat Troops within each Sabre Squadron. Mobility has been a major part of SAS operations since its formation, and new vehicles are regularly tested by the development staff to ensure they meet future requirements with regards to utmost reliability and performance. Currently, the Regiment has two main requirements with regard to its vehicles: mobility on the battlefield and fast and effective transport capable of ferrying the "on call" CRW assault teams from Hereford to the scene of a major incident anywhere in the United Kingdom.

'Range Rovers form the nucleus of the fast-reaction force, being big enough to carry a four-man team, all their equipment and an extensive communications package, while Land Rovers have for years been the Regiment's main off-road vehicle. However, prior to the 1991 Gulf War the land mobility of the Regiment was being given special attention after the request for a purpose-built vehicle had been approved. The resulting trials and development project produced the Light Strike Vehicle (LSV), a two-man, four-wheel drive, all-terrain vehicle. It was undergoing the last phase of its trails in Oman when the Gulf War broke out. Several LSVs are currently being further enhanced, while a second project has concentrated on the procurement of a custom-built Land Rover following its excellent performance in the Gulf. Other vehicles currently under evaluation include a Land Rover Special Operations Vehicle (SOV), a six-wheeled Land Rover used by the Australian SAS, and numerous four-wheel drive vehicles from Europe.'

Land Rovers have been used by the SAS since the 1960s, and they have proved to be remarkable vehicles. Rugged, reliable and able to carry heavy payloads, the Land Rover will continue to serve with the Regiment well into the next century. Pictures of SAS Land Rovers in the Gulf War showed them festooned with a variety of weapons, including Stinger anti-aircraft missiles, Browning heavy machine guns, Milan anti-tank missiles, grenade launchers and general purpose machine guns. The SOV, which is capable of carrying up to six men and all their equipment, also has the capacity to mount a number of weapons, such as machine guns front and rear, an 81mm mortar, a 51mm mortar and personal weapons. In addition, Milan, TOW or a 25mm cannon can be mounted on the pulpit weapons platform.

Though seaborne operations are mainly the preserve of the SBS, SAS Boat Troops also have a maritime brief. This being the case, Hereford is always looking at ways to upgrade the capabilities of its Boat Troops:

'Maritime Counter Measures (MCM) are the priority of the Boat Troops. Working closely with the SBS, their key tasks are the protection of Britain's oilfields from terrorist attacks and the safeguarding of UK shipping anywhere in the world. This is the one area of responsibility the practised in the North Sea in a series of so-called "purple" exercises.

'Among the new developments being examined in the maritime field are heated diving suits and sub-sea vehicles, which are used when exiting a submarine in freezing waters, such as around northern Norway.'

The sub-sea vehicle talked about above is the subskimmer, a piece of equipment that makes a clandestine approach to a hostile shore much easier. The great advantage with this craft is that it can operate as a high-speed surface craft or as a submersible, and can switch from one role to another with ease. On the surface it is powered by an ordinary outboard motor, while below the waves propulsion is provided by two electric underwater motors. An additional feature of the subskimmer is its ability to be 'parked' on the sea bed while the crew completes their mission. Having a maximum surface speed of 25 knots and a top underwater speed of 2.5 knots, the subskimmer will be a great asset to SAS Boat Troops on future operations.

David Stirling believed that his men should be able to arrive at their target by land, sea or air, and ever since the SAS was founded aircraft and parachuting have been an integral part of its operations. Today, the provision of long-range transport aircraft is provided by an RAF Special Forces Flight based at RAF Lyneham, Wiltshire. The principle fixed-wing aircraft used to support SAS operations is the C-130 Hercules long-range transport. There are several attributes that make the Hercules an excellent aircraft for special forces missions. Apart from the fact that it can be refuelled in midair by way of a probe located above the cockpit, it has turboprop propulsion, which means more power for less weight. In addition, high-strength alloys are used in the construction of the aircraft, its tricycle landing gear means it can take off and land from rough airstrips, its radar and full-span thermal de-icing give it an all-weather capacity, and the rear ramp door can be opened in flight for heavy dropping.

Regiment believes is still untested. To date there has been only one major "incident": in 1972, when a combined SAS/SBS team parachuted into the Atlantic Ocean to deal with a bomb threat to the luxury liner *Queen Elizabeth II*. However, the threat turned out to be a hoax, and since then only exercises have been carried out. Nevertheless, the growth in maritime traffic has increased the likelihood of a terrorist incident, and so new security measures have been introduced to prevent this from happening. They are regularly

The Regiment has been trying a number of parachuting concepts in recent years:

'The air wing of development operations is looking towards the twenty-first century with a concept of airborne insertion that will allow a trooper to exit a Hercules at a high altitude up to 80km away from the target. The procedure is called HAHO (high altitude, low opening) and it is already in service. However, at the moment the parachutist has a maximum ceiling of 7600m for leaving the aircraft, and to drift for up to 80km would require him to wear a sophisticated oxygen system and an astronaut-type heated suit to survive the extremely cold temperatures.

'Computer-simulated trials have indicated that such a drop would take up to an hour before the trooper landed, which means the aircraft could remain at a considerable distance away from any enemy detection sources, thus reducing the chances of the operation being compromised. Using a "flat bed", nine-cell steerable canopy, it would be possible to glide across country and land with great accuracy.

'At present the Regiment is also maintaining its HALO (high altitude, low opening) skills, though operationally this form of insertion was turned down by force commanders in the Falklands and the Gulf because they considered it too risky. This being the case, HALO may be downgraded in the future.

'Another futuristic idea being reviewed by the SAS is Icarus, a powered microlight hand glider. The machine, designed by a former RAF officer and first seen at the 1992 Farnborough Air Show, has attracted major interest from the Americans. The concept behind the hi-tech glider is the rescue of special forces soldiers cut off and separated from their teams deep behind enemy lines, a scenario which became a

reality for several SAS soldiers during the 1991 Gulf War. Powered by a 100cc engine, two gliders can be packed into the 2500 litre drop tank of a Tornado aircraft. When assembled and in flight, the Icarus has a top speed of 80km/hr.'

One new form of operations the SAS is being involved in is the fight against drug trafficking:

'The Regiment's role in the 1990s includes an undercover war against international drug gangs. To date the SAS has worked with a number of American drug agencies, such as the Drug Enforcement Agency (DEA), whose personnel have visited Hereford on a number of occasions. Exchange operations have seen SAS men assisting US Coastguard anti-drug patrols. On the domestic front, the Regiment has been involved in drug-busting missions in London, and in one notable case MP5-armed troopers stormed a sea-going tug in docklands and seized a massive narcotics haul. However, in the UK the SAS's greatest interest in the drugs world is in stopping the IRA, who, in the mid-1980s, masterminded a worldwide chain of drug operations to fund its terrorist activities. It also claimed it would defeat the British authorities by undermining the economy with cheap drugs, which would destroy society and cost millions of pounds to put right. This harebrained scheme, needless to say, didn't work, but the IRA's involvement with drug trafficking is real and is one of the SAS's hardest challenges.'

The battle against drugs is a worldwide one and is being fought by many agencies in Europe and the United States. It is a war that is escalating in intensity: world production of opium doubled between 1986 and 1989, and the cocaine trade has wrecked many governments in Latin America, most notably Colombia. The main market for drugs is still the United States, which seems to have an insatiable desire for cocaine, heroin and marijuana, but increasingly Europe is attracting the attention of the world's drug

Left: HAHO parachuting. Such techniques will give the SAS even greater flexibility for future missions.

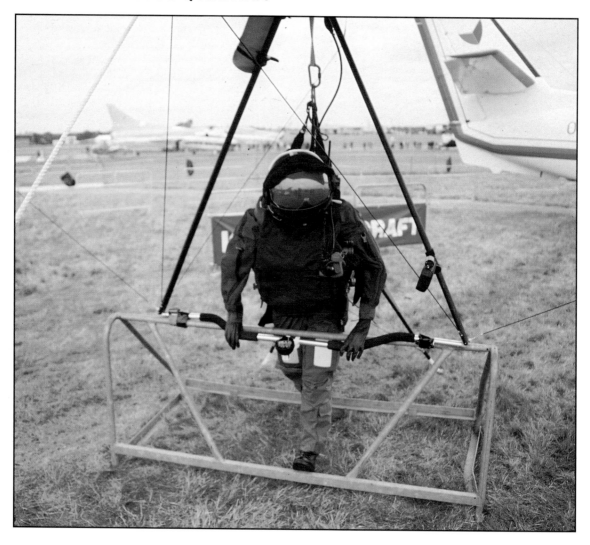

Above: The new Icarus glider, which, if it had been in service, might have prevented the deaths of SAS soldiers during the 1991 Gulf War with Iraq.

barons. As a consequence, drugs have started to pour onto the continent, and the inner cities of western Europe in particular have become major distribution points for narcotics. At long last the state's agencies have been mobilised, and they include the SAS. But the enemy is powerful

The Colombian cocaine trade developed from a small cottage industry in the early 1970s into a multi-billion dollar concern by the beginning of the 1990s, with its own distribution network and armies of 'narco-terrorists' to ensure the trade continued undisturbed. The

chief villain of the piece is the Medellin Cartel, a loose association of drug producers and smugglers who have combined to share the market, ward off rivals and intimidate the government. The Cartel's profits are immense, and with this wealth has come the power to kill the country's presidents, judges, senior army officials and a multitude of civilians with impunity. To be fair to the Colombian government, measures have been taken against the Cartel, but it has proved to be an intractable foe. In the late 1980s Western leaders, such as President George Bush of the United States and Prime Minister Thatcher of the UK, tried to help the Colombians against the Cartel. Thatcher, for example, sent an SAS team to

Above: No one doubts that international drug gangs pose a threat to Western democracy, and so units such as the SAS have been tasked to fight them. But is it a case of too little too late?

assist in the war against cocaine production in the Colombian jungle. It was an astute move: the SAS has a fine pedigree in jungle warfare. The troopers trained a unit called the Anti-Narcotics Police in the art of jungle warfare, teaching them such things as carrying rifles when on patrol crooked in the forearms, in a position known as the 'Belfast cradle', that allows a quicker response when a surprise contact with the enemy occurs. In a significant victory over the drug barons, an SAS-led team found and killed one of

Colombia's leading cocaine barons, Gonzalo Rodriquez Gacha, along with his son and five bodyguards. As ever, though, there were other ruthless drug lords to replace Gacha. One of the major drug barons, Pablo Escobar, surrendered to the government, but on his own terms. In effect both sides declared a draw, but the export of cocaine to the United States and Europe goes on. The SAS, for its part, continues to train Colombian police and military units in the art of jungle warfare, but one wonders how long this deployment will go on for in the face of UK defence cuts and the continuing over-stretching of the Regiment's resources. One thing is certain: the SAS's campaign against international drug gangs is just beginning.

SAS OPERATIONS 1941 TO THE PRESENT

1941
Axis airfields raided:
14 December:
Agheila   Enemy vehicles destroyed

21 December:
Agedabia   37 Axis aircraft destroyed

1942
Axis airfields raided:
8 March:
Barce   One aircraft and some trucks destroyed
Berka   15 aircraft destroyed

25 March:
Benina   Five aircraft destroyed

13 June:
Benina   Two aircraft destroyed
Berka   11 aircraft destroyed

7 July:
Bagoush   37 Axis aircraft destroyed
El Daba   Failed to destroy any aircraft
Fuka   14 aircraft destroyed

12 July:
Fuka   22 aircraft destroyed

26 July:
Sidi Haneish   40 aircraft destroyed

1943
12 July:
Operation 'Chestnut'   2 SAS
Abortive operation in northern Sicily intended to support the Allied invasion of the island

3 September:
Operation 'Baytown'   Special Raiding Squadron (1 SAS temporarily renamed) Capture of the Italian port of Bagnara

7 September:
Operation 'Speedwell'   2 SAS
Successful mission in northeast Italy

2-6 October:
Operation 'Begonia'   2 SAS
Evacuation of British POWs from Italy

27 October:
Operation 'Candytuft'   2 SAS
Railway line cut on east Italian coast

1944
7 January:
Operation 'Maple'   2 SAS
Abortive attempt to support the Anzio landings

30 January:
Operation 'Baobab'   2 SAS
Support of the Anzio landings in Italy

6 June:
Operation 'Titanic'   1 SAS
Unsuccessful mission in Normandy

6 June-3 July:
Operation 'Bulbasket'   1 SAS
Railway lines cut and trains destroyed in southern France

6 June:
Operation 'Dingson'   4 SAS
Abortive mission in Brittany, France

6-9 June:
Operation 'Samwest'   4 SAS
Mission in Brittany that was disrupted by German forces

6-21 June:
Operation 'Houndsworth'   1 SAS
Railway lines cut west of Dijon, France

Above: David Stirling, whose vision and drive established the world's most effective special forces unit. Stirling himself died in 1990.

6 June-15 August:
Operation 'Gain'   1 SAS
German commuications severed
southwest of Paris

7 June:
Operation 'Cooney'   4 SAS
Severing railway lines in Brittany, France,
before joining up with the 'Dingson' party

23 June-18 July:
Operation 'Lost'   4 SAS
A very successful mission in Brittany, France,
which resulted in over 2000 enemy casualties
and a large number of *Maquis* being armed

8 July-11 August:
Operation 'Haft'   1 SAS
Intelligence gathering in northwest France

16 July-7 October:
Operation 'Dickens'   3 SAS
Disruption of rail communications around
Nantes, France.

19 July-23 August:
Operation 'Defoe'   2 SAS
Ineffectual reconnaissance of the Argentan area
of Normandy

23 July-10 September:
Operation 'Rupert'   2 SAS
Unsuccessful attempt to destroy rail lines in
eastern France

25 July:
Operation 'Gaff'   2 SAS
Abortive attempt to kill Erwin Rommel

27 July-1 September:
Operation 'Hardy'   2 SAS
Aggressive raiding around Dijon

28 July-15 August:
Operation 'Chaucer'   5 SAS
General harassment of German forces in
northwest France

31 July-15 August:
Operation 'Shakespeare'   5 SAS
Harassment of German forces west of Paris

3-15 August:
Operation 'Bunyan'   5 SAS
Harassing German forces west of Paris

3-24 August:
Operation 'Dunhill'   2 SAS
Intelligence gathering in
northwest France

5-18 August:
Operation 'Derry'   3 SAS
German forces hindered as they tried
to move towards Brest

10-23 August:
Operation 'Haggard'   1 SAS
Fighting German forces around the River Loire

10 August-27 September:
Operation 'Samson'   3 SAS
Moderately successful mission in southern
France

11-24 August:
Operation 'Marshall'   3 SAS
Offensive operations in France

12 August-9 October:
Operation 'Loyton'   2 SAS
Intelligence gathering in eastern France

13-24 August:
Operation 'Snelgrove'   3 SAS
Arming Resistance forces in southern France

13 August-19 September:
Operation 'Barker'   3 SAS
Protecting flank of US Third Army
as it advanced through France

13 August-24 September:
Operation 'Harrod'   3 SAS
Disrupting enemy movements in
central France

13 August-26 September:
Operation 'Kipling'   1 SAS
Large jeep operation in central France which
resulted in the surrender of 3000 Germans

15 August-9 September:
Operation 'Jockworth'   3 SAS
Disrupting enemy forces in
southeast France

16 August-13 September:
Operation 'Noah'   5 SAS
Intelligence gathering in the French Ardennes

19 August-11 September:
Operation 'Newton'   3 SAS
Successful harassing mission of German forces
in central France

Above: SAS jeeps in northwest Europe, 1945. One of the largest SAS jeep missions in this period was Operation 'Archway', which involved 75 jeeps.

19 August-19 September:
Operation 'Wallace'   2 SAS
Large, successful jeep operation around Dijon, western France

26 August-3 September:
Operation 'Wolsey'
Intelligence gathering in northeast France

28 August-1 September:
Operation 'Benson'   5 SAS
Intelligence gathering in northeast France

29 August-14 September:
Operation 'Spenser'   4 SAS
Much damage inflicted in the Germans in central France

2 September-15 September:
Operation 'Brutus'   5 SAS
Intelligence gathering in Belgian Ardennes

6-11 September:
Operation 'Caliban'   5 SAS
Severing enemy communications in northeast Belgium

15 September-3 October:
Operation 'Pistol'   2 SAS
Cutting rail lines in eastern France

16 September-14 March 1945:
Operation 'Fabian'   5 SAS
Intelligence gathering around Arnhem, Holland

27 September-17 March 1945:
Operation 'Gobbo'   5 SAS
Intelligence gathering around Drente, Holland

24 December-25 January 1945:
Operation 'Franklin'   4 SAS
Supporting US forces during German Ardenness offensive

27 December-14 February 1945:
Operation 'Galia'   2 SAS
Intelligence gathering in northern Italy

27 December-15 January 1945:
Operation 'Regent'   5 SAS
Blunting the German Ardennes offensive

1945
March-May 1945:
Operation 'Archway'   1 and 2 SAS
Assisting advance of British 21st Army Group
into Germany

4 March-24 April:
Operation 'Tombola'   2 SAS
Successful offensive mission in north Italy

3-18 April:
Operation 'Keystone'   2 SAS
Jeep mission in Holland

3 April-8 May:
Operation 'Larkswood'   5 SAS
Jeep offensive into northern Germany

6 April-6 May:
Operation 'Howard'   1 SAS
Jeep operation in northwest Germany

May:
Operation 'Apostle'
Disarming German garrison in Norway

1950-60
Malaya
Campaign against communist guerrillas in
the jungle which resulted in the
reformation of 22 SAS

November 1958-January 1959
Jebel Akhdar, Oman
Successful campaign against rebels
in northern Oman

1963-1966
Borneo   A, B, D and G Squadrons
Victorious jungle campaign against rebel
guerrillas and Indonesian forces

April 1964-November 1967
Aden   A, B and D Squadrons
Campaign against tribesmen in the Radfan area

of the interior, and guerrillas in the port of
Aden itself (so-called 'Keeni Meeni' operations)

1969-
Northern Ireland
On-going campaign against terrorists in Ulster

1970-76
Oman
Successful campaign against communist
guerrillas, included very effective SAS 'hearts
and minds' policy

19 July 1972
The Battle of Mirbat
Nine-man SAS team defeats large guerrilla
force in Oman during one-day battle

5 May 1980
Iranian Embassy, London
Operation 'Nimrod'
Successful SAS hostage-rescue operation

July 1981
The Gambia
SAS helps to restore President Jawara to power

April-June 1982
The Falkland Islands
Intelligence gathering and raiding operations
against Argentinian positions

8 May 1987
Loughall, Northern Ireland
SAS wipes out East Tyrone Brigade in ambush

6 March 1988
Gibraltar
SAS team shoots dead three IRA terrorists

1989-
Columbia
22 SAS committed to the anti-cocaine war. This
commitment is on-going

August 1990-February 1991
Arabian Gulf
Large SAS contingent involved in operations
behind the lines in Iraq and Kuwait

INDEX